SEVENTH EDITION

A COLLECTION OF WORKS BY TEENS FOR
TEENS, TEACHERS & OUR COMMUNITIES

STEPHEN F. AUSTIN STATE UNIVERSITY PRESS
2016

Copy Writer: Sarah Rafael García
Logo Design: Jimmy Prieto

Copyright © 2016 by Barrio Writers

Published by Stephen F. Austin State University Press
1936 North Street, LAN 203
P.O. Box 13007
Nacogdoches, Texas 75962
sfapress@sfasu.edu
sfasu.edu/sfapress
936-468-1078

All rights reserved. No part of this publication may be reproduced, stored in a retrieval system or transmitted in any form or by any means - for example, elextronic, photocopy, and recording - without the prior written permission of the publisher. The only exception is brief quotations in printed reviews.

ISBN: 978-1-62288- 167-3

TABLE OF CONTENTS

Tierra Harris	11
Jose Vega	14
Johnny Montaño	17
Miguel Del Castillo	19
Daniel Wilder	22
Karen Guadalupe Muñoz	25
Jocelyn Sanchez	27
Cristian Dominguez	30
Marlen Gallegos	33
Diana Angelica De La Riva	42
Adamaris Ramirez	44
Graciella Castillo	46
Anonymous Barrio Writer	48
Alyssa Richards	50
Noemi Ocampo	52
Matthew Lopez	54
Kaiden Brown	60
Rosalinda Segura	63
Miakoda Earley	67
Jennifer Belen Alvarez	70
Gabriella Isget	74
Belen Mendoza	79
Joanna Elizabeth Santos	83
Kevin Organista	87
Luis Flores	90
Marcella Espinoza	92
Jesús I'x Nazario	94
Petra Jasmin Herrera	97
Hannah Hinojosa	99

Lily Risk	102
Jasmine Capello	104
Diego Montaño	106
Carlos Amaya	109
Armani Scott	111
Jake Malvaiz	116
Mireya Del Rocio Ortiz	119
Leslie Lawyer	121
Catheryne Molina	123
Diana Hernandez	127
Ariana Espinoza	129
Tobin Gonzales Mahlke	131
Odalis Espinoza	133
Diego Flores	135
Maricarmen Velazquez	140
Lizeth Hilario Echeverria	142
Eligio Cisneros	145
Marcelo Martinez	147
Erick Romero Chavez	149
Rosie Lawyer	151
Karla Moreno	153
Jacob Paul Castillo	155
Vanessa Marcos	157
Karina Mendez	159
Elizabeth Marcos	161
Jesse Castillo	163
Joana Tello	165
Alfredo Marcos	167
Midnight Amber Smith	169
Monica Hernandez	171
John Anthony Muñoz	174

Darlene Ayala	176
Jenna Abshire	179
Adrian Martinez	181
Jazmin Condado	183
CJ Sounds	185
Sapphire Sea	191
Chris Sida	193
Melanie Elaine Salazar	195
K.J. Huey	197
Judith Araziry	202
Alexa Smith	209
Arnolg Garcilazo	212
Shyla Driver	214
Galilea Marcos	217
Phoenix Conditt	221
Marilynn Montaño	224

Writing Advisor's Note

Barrio Writers is more than a workshop; it is a community. Barrio Writers is a community of youth and adult mentors who believe in each other and the power of thoughts and words anchored in lived experience.

"Own your words," we would often say while collaborating as a group. "Never sell yourself short or apologize for who you are." Simple phrases to say but challenging lessons to truly follow, even as adults. How often, for example, have we censored ourselves out of concern for what others might think or how they might react to us? How often have we limited our writing to the rules of the classroom to make the grade or graduate? And how often have we held our tongue rather than unleash our real opinion, nervous that we might make a mistake, look silly, or face hostility from those who want to define and stereotype us? Barrio Writers is about claiming our identity in all its complexity without shame and proclaiming that we will be HEARD. That youth especially deserve to be heard and included as leaders of change and creativity in the broader communities we are continually building.

The members of Barrio Writers come from so many places and different situations of struggle and triumph. They bring their personal histories to the workshop's lessons every single day, and they support each other by encouraging their peers to stretch beyond what they—or perhaps others—may believe they are capable of. Throughout an intensive week of readings, writing, and presentations, the youth create their own unique pieces to share at a public reading. The raw honesty and depth of these pieces convey many of the questions, dreams, doubts, and visions that these youth have carried inside them all along. Indeed, they have always had a voice, but it is we who have not been listening closely enough if we are surprised by their abilities and keen feelings.

It has been a lot of fun to work alongside these Barrio Writers as I have come to know them as individuals. The kindness, strength, and sense of justice they have demonstrated to me during our time together have blown me away on this learning journey, and I feel grateful to have been part of such a special community of writers. For youth in a safe space to speak openly, work through the ups and downs of life, and explore who they are and what they stand for, Barrio Writers is an incredibly precious and important project that deserves our support. Keep on rocking the world with your truth, Barrio Writers of the past, present, and future!

—Aileen Ford
M.A. student in Latin American Studies
and Public Affairs at University of Texas at Austin

Barrio Writers Writing Advisor,
Austin, Texas, Summer 2015

Preface

Barrio Writers (BW) is a creative writing program founded by author Sarah Rafael García, which provides free college level writing workshops to teenagers in underserved communities. In the summer of 2009, thirty students came together to form the first Barrio Writers chapter in Santa Ana, California, a non-profit reading and writing program that aims to empower teens through creative writing, higher education, and cultural arts.

Barrio Writers is a non-profit program that offers workshops and additional one-on-one tutor hours for one week throughout the academic summer break. Students receive college-level workshops to build skills in reading, grammar, creative writing, critical-thinking and freedom of expression through cultural arts. The session includes guest writers who serve as role models in our neighborhoods and support youth aspirations.

The Barrio Writers program thrives through its community collaboration. By aligning with universities and Resistencia Bookstore, Barrio Writers participants are exposed to diverse activities provided in the surrounding areas while in turn give support to the local cultural arts and community resources. Most recently we partnered with Stephen F. Austin State University in Nacogdoches, Texas and the Mexican American Studies Student Organization at the University of Houston. Both chapters united to form a new community of Barrio Writers along our long-standing chapter in Santa Ana, California, which was hosted by El Centro Cultural de Mexico, and our second chapter at the University of Texas at Austin.

The program strives to present alternative forms of expressions through cultural art collaboration in the community. The summer workshops culminate with a live reading, which allows Barrio Writers to present final pieces to our community and reach a wider audience by potential media coverage and book sales. The written works submitted by teens from the multiple chapters are published in an anthology collection. It is our goal to include all chapters in each annual edition to form a diverse youth community beyond the workshops.

Barrio Writers participants are between the ages of thirteen to nineteen-years-old and reside in the surrounding area of the local chapters. By opening workshops to all levels of students from local schools and neighborhoods, Barrio Writers includes teenagers from diverse circumstances to participate and share their lives with our society. We also encourage for college and university students up to the age of twenty-one-years-old to participate as peers obtaining higher education.

One goal of the program is to publish an anthology collection of written works demonstrating the diverse backgrounds of teenagers that can be used in and out of the classroom. *Barrio Writers* is a collection of works by teens for teens, teachers and our communities. All profits from the book are returned to the Barrio Writers program for future years. The long-term goal is to publish a new edition each year with hopes that more neighborhoods will adopt the program and more teachers will use the BW book in the classroom. The Barrio Writers program and its annual anthology are designed to empower the teenage community while establishing a self-sufficient educational program that will represent community pride, perseverance, and endless possibilities for following generations.

Tierra Harris

Tierra (Tee Tee) Harris is 17 years old and was born on April 14, 1998. She grew up in 3rd Ward Yellowstone, Houston, TX. Tierra is the oldest and only girl out of 3 children. Although she was born in one of the most dangerous neighborhoods in Houston, she acts way different from those who grew up there. Not saying it is a good or bad thing, but her personality is usually not what people expect. Tierra currently plays volleyball, basketball, softball, is in National Honors Society, FCCLA, Academic Achievers and a 2016 class officer. She also served as class President for her freshman and sophomore year. Tierra's aspiration in life is to own her own children's rec center, take over her family music business, and inspire teens like herself.

Heal the World

It's time to heal the world and it's something a Band-Aid can't fix.
Even though segregation is over the world has gotten worse.
Not necessarily through actions but their thoughts in their minds and the emotions in their hearts
I walk into high school the first day and I'm nervous
Girls walking by mugging because I'm "mean"
The volleyball team don't like me because I'm "ghetto"
Teachers not giving me eye contact because I feel "left out"
And the only reason Ms. Smith and Ms. Lewis like me is because I'm black.

But how do you even know that about me?
Is it because I'm black?
I am not a walking stereotype.
I do not live in the box statistics have created.
Just because I am colored does not mean I will have a baby at 16 and live off the government.
Just because I am dark does not mean I'm wild and ignorant.
Just because I speak proper does not mean I am boujie.
Just because I am BLACK
Does not mean if you disagree with me my only way to handle it is by cursing you out rolling my neck and clap to a beat.
My best friends are Hispanic, I know who my dad is, and I live in the suburbs
So do yourself a favor, forget the statistics
Take your mind out of every race has to be a certain way.
There's only one race, the human race.
But unfortunately the world won't be healed until we kill the enemy: us.

Why do I have to be an "Oreo"?

Why do I have to be an "Oreo"?
Because I don't fit the harsh stereotype?
Is there even a certain way I should act?
Are you saying blacks have to act a certain way?
 And whites have to act a certain way?

Why do I have to be an "Oreo"?
Is that even a bad thing?
Is there such thing as acting "white"?
Are you saying white is better?
Do I have to be ignorant to be black?

Why do I have to be an "Oreo"?
Is it because I'm not ghetto?
Or not ghetto enough?

Why can't I just be Tierra?
The girl who speaks properly, educated, and doesn't see color.

Writing Activity

1. A stereotype is a widely held but fixed and oversimplified image or idea of a person that aims to take away their humanity. Have you been called any stereotype? Which one(s)? How are they not true? Write a poem or story where you challenge that stereotype.

2. How many different communities do you fit into or have connections with? How do you fit into them? How do you not? Write about how you can connect all those communities.

3. How does race play into your life? Is it negative, positive, both, or neither? How? Write a story taking place in a day where race has affected you.

Jose Vega

My name is Jose Vega. I'm in the 7th grade going to the 8th grade. I'm Hispanic. I have lived in Nacogdoches. I have two younger brothers and one older brother. I have won three awards in music and two awards in academics. My dreams are to become an Inventor/Businessman.

Mission Destruction of Government
Novel Excerpt

"Agent John I know that was your last mission but I need you to do something else." Said the Director. "Do I really have to do this?" said agent John. "Your mission is to assassinate the president". "What!" screamed John? "We have intel that the president has begun his plan for world domination".

Later that week: "This is your team Amanda Smith Master of Disguise, Robert Collins Tech Wizard, and finally James Stevens the guard" said the director.

THE PLAN: James sneaks Robert and John into the security office. Robert releases the virus to get control of all cameras and computers. John climbs into the air vent system to get down to the presidents office. Amada dresses as a member of the president's cabinet and distract the president. There is an air vent behind the president's chair John will drop in. Amanda will hold the president down then John shoots the president.

DAY 1 Saturday 2 weeks till the assassination

Amanda is sitting at her desk trying to figure out what to wear to the on the night of the assassination. "Robert!" screams John. "WHAT" responds Robert while programming the virus. "How do you plan to get into the security room to release the virus?" asked John. "Why are you asking me," said Robert , "James is the one who is going to get us in". "Well how do you know he's not going to tell the president about our plan to assassinate him?" "James is a fake guard" said Amanda frustrated. "Jeez woman calm down" said James walking in then Robert and John kept arguing. Amanda started screaming at James saying she was calm.

"Everybody Shut Up," screamed the Director, "We need to prepare for the assassination it is only two weeks away Amanda find the dress by tomorrow you have more work to do. John listen James isn't going to tell the president he swore but if he does tell he will be brought here starved, tortured, poisoned, stabbed, and shot. Robert finish up that virus we don't have time to be arguing with John. Everybody listen the assassination is on Saturday the president is having a party at the White House the president will be too busy to attend the party he will be in his office finalizing his plans. James there will be a lot of cameras and other guards in the White House so it will be hard to get them in just think about that. Amanda to get into the White House you will need an ID Robert will be in charge of making it now everybody start working we have two long weeks ahead of us."

Writing Activity

1. What is your favorite sci-fi (science fiction) movie? What about your favorite sci-fi book? Did you know sci-fi movies and books purposely include social commentary in their plots?

    Social commentary is the act of using writing or films to provide commentary on issues in a society. This is often done with the idea of creating or promoting change by telling the general public about a given problem and getting people to see the sense in justice.

    Plot: *noun*, the main events of a play, novel, movie, or similar work, devised and presented by the writer as an interrelated sequence.

2. Now reread, Jose's novel excerpt. What do you think is the social commentary in his story? What other types of stories does it remind you of? What are their social commentaries and/or plots? What lesson are they trying to teach the reader/audience?
3. Like Jose, think of something in society you want to comment on, something you feel strongly or confused about (racism, gender issues, poverty). Now, use sci-fi and flash-fiction to write about it. Try to only write a story under 500 words. 500 words is roughly one page, single-spaced.

> **Science Fiction:** fiction based on imagined future scientific or technological advances and major social or environmental changes, frequently portraying space or time travel and life on other planets.

Johnny Montaño

Johnny Montaño is a shy 10-year-old boy who loves to read, write and school. He does not like to play that much or talk to kids. His sister Marilynn convinced him to go to Barrio Writers to write more. Reading is his best thing but when he went to Barrio Writers he discovered that writing is his best thing too.

Police Man

Day and night polices search above and below for someone who robs a store, kidnaps people or kill people. Police man do the same thing they kill people, go too fast, yell, bring people to jail and sometimes kill people because they are mad. Who is the real criminal? Policeman or people on the street? My opinion is that the real criminal is the police man. When I was walking with my mother and lots of people were looking what had happened so policeman yelled at us for looking. On the news I heard a policeman kidnap a boy and tied him up. If policeman keep us safe then why are they killing people? Are they mad?

Being Embarrassed

Being embarrassed is when your mother comes to your school unexpected, your friend telling lies about you or when you pee your pants in school.

However, for me it is when your friend tells lies about you. When they say lies about you, I feel like they are not my friend and that they are using me. That has happened to me before so I just ignore them and pretend they are not my friend.

Being Shy

Kids are shy when they go to a new school, join new programs or saying a speech. Every once in a while people get shy then it goes away and you feel like you have them. When you are not shy you start to talk and raise your hand. Every once in a while you still get shy even though you think you are not shy.

Writing Activity

1. Discuss with your group the areas you live in. What are the differences and similarities? How does the media report about where the area you live in? Is it positive or negative?

2. Does your neighborhood get patrolled constantly? How does it make you feel? Write your first experience with a police officer—good or bad—there's not only one story.

Miguel Del Castillo

Miguel Del Castillo is a 19-year-old, middle-child born on July 1, 1996 and a high school graduate of the Class of 2015. His favorite things are listening to hip-hop and Mexican music, jugar futbol con sus amigos y ayudar a su familia. He wants to make music for a living because he wants to inspire the next generation by making music and send a message that they can understand, to be a young voice for them. El quiere ayudar a la gente joven para que no dejan de creer en la vida. Que trabajen duro para vivir sus sueños y ayuden a sus familias. He wants to show everyone that you can do anything if you set your mind to it and know that nothing is impossible, just believe you can, that's what he goes by in life everyday. So don't listen to anyone that says you're nothing. He wants to be the one, that voice everybody hears and can inspire. He is Miguel Del Castillo and he says, "Yes we can! ¡Si se puede!"

Don't Worry

Why me what did I do to deserve this?
I keep on repeating those
words to myself.

A new year is starting
finally senior year, I hope I can get

through this year without any problems.
Three months have passed.
No, not again I'm shaking.
Heart beating fast and the feeling
of panic starts.

What should I do? I feel hopeless.
No matter what, I can't give up.

One week of school left.
Thank you Jesus I knew I could
make it through, I just wish my dad was here.
But I know he is proud of me.

June 5, 2015 Graduation Day
Thank you God for helping me through
this year, for giving me strength.
I go to my family and thank them for always
being there and supporting me.

Since then, I wake up thinking about life,
it's just the time to start a new chapter.

Never 2 Late

Stand up young soldier don't you dare give up
Wake up get up
Get your mind ready
Never 2 late you better get started
Cause life is just beginning
Never 2 late to speak your mind
Never 2 late to take chance in life
Forget what they say stop thinking about it
Go for it this is your chance take it
Before it's gone
Never 2 late to speak your mind
Never 2 late to take a chance in life
Stay strong young soldier believe
You can tell yourself that

Forget what they say
Never 2 late to speak your mind
Never 2 late to take a chance in life
Be strong don't give up cause
You may become the next big thing
The one to change the world to
Start a new generation
Stay strong young soldier don't you dare give up
Wake up get up get your mind ready because
Your name could be next in history.

<u>Writing Activity</u>
1. What plans do you have after high school? (It's ok if you don't know yet, but maybe share a dream you hope to reach.) What keeps you motivated to keep reaching your goals?

2. Miguel is the first in his family to graduate from high school. It was definitely a hard journey for him due to many reasons out of his control. Write a "Dear Miguel" letter, or maybe choose to write yourself a letter to help you get through your own tough times. Miguel chose poetry to write such a letter to himself. Be creative when you choose words to motivate him or yourself to keep going. Maybe even add some music or hip-hop beats to it!

Daniel Wilder

So Daniel Wilder was born in either June or July of the year 2000. From what I can tell he likes to act and play his saxophone and stuff like that. He's got that whole angsty artist thing going on, a real teenager's teenager, y'know? He's alright though. Like, one time he lent me 5 bucks and didn't even want it back. I dunno, sometimes he can be pretty obnoxious though. Nevermind. I mean, it's just that... Nevermind. Um, well he asked us to uh thank his mother for driving him around and just generally being pretty supportive. He also wants to thank his sister for supporting him by going 5 hours away for the duration of this writing camp. Oh, and he wants to thank Werner Herzog. What a fantastic filmmaker.

The Leaves: A Romp on How White I Am

He was only nineteen.

As a victim on the top of the food chain,
I weep because it was the palms of my hands,
Around and around until there he lay,
Limp and lame.

And wouldn't it be nice,
To pretend the sands would stand to help,

Indulging and holding our time more than theirs,
As if the favored child wasn't just privileged.

And I acknowledge the progress we've made,
But some see those leaps and bounds
As muted sounds to be carried away
In handcuffs.

No blood gets on the cuffs of my sleeves as I wash my hands from the blame because I'm just
Drawn this way,
Drawn towards a higher taste only I can completely savor.

A savior
Martyr behavior
Leads to an understanding of the strange fruit
I have made
And the people that have laid
Their lives down so I could frown and think
It was all in bad taste.

Making the love we have into an odyssey,
Into a pair, two working in tandem,
And married to a policy
A helping hound
That the police have found
Under our bedlam,
And in our bedrooms,
And in the closet,
And under the floorboards,

And so if he was stabbed because of the way he was dyed,
He died with the knife in my hand and a smile in my eyes,
Because I know no one's really there,
Grinning because I know no one really cares.

Writing Activity
1. What do you know about "white privilege?" How would you define it? Do you think all "white" people are privileged? Why or why not? Do you think privilege exists in other groups of people? How so?
2. Do you believe all people can create change? Or do some people in society have more power than others? What is the difference between "power" and "empowerment"? What are some groups you "empower" but are not part of through identity? How do you "empower" them?

3. Like, Daniel, choose a group you want to empower and write a narrative that you think will help bring the issue into conversations with your own group (race, ethnicity, socioeconomic status, gender, religion). Be creative! Write a poem in similar style to your favorite writer. Daniel chose Allen Ginsberg, who will you choose? Maybe Aracelis Girmay, Beyoncé, Chingo Bling, Ocean Vuong or maybe a satire comic artist like Lalo Alcaraz? If you don't know who these artists are, just Google them and check out their work. ☺

Karen Guadalupe Muñoz

Karen Guadalupe Muñoz is a Mexican 15-year-old teen born in Austin, Texas. She is the oldest of three girls and will be the first generation in the family to attend college. She aspires to go to Baylor University and get in the medical school. She also wants to strive to become a professional soccer player. She spends her summer days at Breakthrough volunteering for middle school students. She is very proud of her culture, enough to walk around UT playing loud Mexican music with her friends.

My Statement of Purpose

I would change the world by proving to all those people who are against Mexican immigration and show them that we are people who succeed. Not just some rapists, killers, or drug dealers. Mexicans can make a change to the society; they are the base of production. We've helped and made things for them and they still hate us.

What are they going to do when we leave? Are they just going to say they will give us equal rights but overtime it will be unequal as usual but this time it's going to be worse! Making us slaves and repeating history once again, but that will not get that far as some people will think. My people will not just sit and watch their horrible life pass by. One strong leader will take them and defend the rights that Mexicans deserve and not be treated unfairly. In return for what they make, pick, package, or deliver to the white clean hands that just talk on the phone and stay relaxed in their big houses. Most Mexicans don't come to the U.S. to ruin other people's life they are trying to start fresh and give a better life to their families.

I will start with myself working hard to get in a high position in the medical field and from there I will start an organization that will help Latino kids who want to succeed in life and are willing to try and make a difference. Then the government and all those people who doubt us will have a smack to the face by our accomplishment that we can be smart, we can be successful, and we can be just like them.

Writing Activity
1. In her work, Karen refers to racist rhetoric that conservative politicians, specifically Republican Presidential Candidate Donald Trump, use to influence the opinions of their voters. What do you think the effect of that rhetoric is? Have you or people in your community been affected by it?

    Write an opinion piece on how you think the racist rhetoric of politicians and other high profile figures in the media affect public opinion and action, including personal examples.

    Additional resource: Listen to NPR's Latino USA episode and consider how it relates to Karen's work and the discussion question: https://soundcloud.com/latinousa/sets/1609-sticks-stones

2. Sometimes the ways in which we want to enact change begin with our personal dreams, and taking care of ourselves. Write a list of things you wish to do or accomplish in your lifetime, and consider how they may help or affect others. This could help you respond to activity 3.

3. The possibility to change situations, laws, and systems is what inspires many youth to work towards a better future. Using the prompt that Karen responded to, how would you change the world? What would you focus on and why? Write a statement of purpose in response to this question, and make it personal. Just as Karen wrote passionately about her goals, so too should you.

    > **Statement of purpose** is a short essay or statement, usually relating to an academic application that describes what and why you wish to do something.

Jocelyn Sanchez

My name is Jocelyn Sanchez. I am four feet eleven inches tall and my doctor says that this will be my adult height because shortness runs in my family. I have curly brown hair that was given to me by my father and I have had braces in the past. I attend Godinez Fundamental High School and I will be an incoming sophomore in the fall. I am currently 14 years of age. I was born on August 24, 2000 at four in the afternoon. My mom's name is Maricruz and my dad's name is Javier. They are both from Mexico, my mom is from El Grullo, Jalisco and my dad is from Cuautla, Morelos. They met here in the U.S and in 1996 had my older brother Joshua. Like every other traditional Mexican familia, mine too is very big. On both my mother and father's side I have numerous aunts, uncles, and cousins. I have various types of favorite foods that range from Chinese to Mexican to Italian but my all-time favorite food is cheese, I cannot live without it! By strangers I can seem shy but the truth is, I talk A LOT. My mind is constantly thinking and having conversations of its own but people are too busy to notice or to even care because they too are immersed in their own thoughts. Just as much as I like talk, I also love to dance Ballet Folklorico. In my ballet Folklorico dance class, I always look forward to the annual dance showcase because preforming brings me such great satisfaction. In the future I plan to go to a four year university and graduate. Even though I am yet not certain of what career to study, I hope to be successful in whatever it is I decide to do.

Trash

My feet are covered by the warm sand and my hair sways backwards as I am hit by the cool breeze. I stand looking out towards the ocean lost in my thoughts when suddenly I am called back to reality by my mother who ushers me to hurry up. It is dusk, my mother, father, and I are at the beach collecting cans. It's dirty and exhausting but it's my allowance money. I speed up to the next trash can as the only thing I want is to go home and sleep. I begin to search for cans and soon enough a blue eyed blonde girl in between the ages of 8-10 walks up to me. She's dressed in clothes that are nicer than mine and shoes that look fairly new. She examines what I'm doing. It's not long before her high pitched voice fills my ears as she says, "Why are you picking trash?" It takes me a moment to register her question, but when I fully do I realize that I am now very angry. I say nothing. I am so mad that I can feel the tears well up in my eyes. I try to think of a comeback but nothing comes to mind. As I didn't know who to blame. It's been about three minutes now and I still haven't said anything. Once she realizes that I am not going to answer her question she leaves. I continue to stand there still thinking of who or what to blame but I soon realize that its useless for there is no one to blame. Only someone who can understand.

The Start

My interest in writing first sparked when I received a compliment for my writing in the second grade. The whole class was assigned to write about apples. Everyone wrote and when they thought it was good enough they showed it to our teacher Mrs. Peralta. Unfortunately for them it wasn't good enough so she sent them back. I had finished writing and my paper was just sitting on my desk. I was terrified of showing it to her and being rejected. I didn't want to risk being told to go back and re do it, even though now I know it's a good thing. In the back of my mind I knew I had to be a woman about it and show her what I had written. So I did I stood up pushed in my chair and began to walk up to her. I held my breath. Thinking of turning back and just pretend like I don't finish but my legs had already reached her desk and she'd seen me. I handed her my paper. I was so scared. I tried to study her face so id figure out what thoughts were crossing her mind but her head was tilted down. She finished and the part I feared the most was approaching, the feedback. She looked up, her eyes met mine. I was biting my tongue in anticipation waiting for her response. After what felt like an eternity she smiled warmly at me and said with a gentle voice, "It was good". Phew, I was relieved. With that being said I hurried back scared that she might change her mind. Since then it was those three little words, "it was good" were the ones that sparked an interest in me. Even though those three little words may not seem so great or powerful they were to eight year old me. It was the start.

Writing Activity
1. Is there a moment you felt embarrassed? How did you overcome it and why is it important to go through embarrassing moments to reach your end goal?

2. Do you like writing? Do you keep a journal? Keep a journal by your nightstand and write last thoughts of the day or early thoughts of the morning for one week. At the end of the week, read over all your journal entries and write reflections about your entries along with the process. Did you find that you're writing changed?

Cristian Dominguez

I'm Cristian Dominguez. The third of the family. Most people think that I was a very violent person because of my identity. I have faced discrimination a lot. I don't hang with kids much unless I'm at school, but if it's a bad person I stay away.

One day in First grade two boys were bullying me. It was the end of the school day. Everyone was watching, nobody seemed to care about me. Now to 6th grade, most people have weed especially people who don't care for others much. So I try to not hang with them. Most people from school use FTP which means f*ck the police. I get really pissed off when I see it and when I see people stick their stupid ass middle finger. Most get caught and go to ALC. I never want to talk to them.

I never got much support. I only get it from a few people. Once the girl who I thought was my friend turned out to be a fake-ass. She just didn't care about the world. Well, the fake-ass started bullying a friend on Facebook. I was helping my friend survive the bullying because the fake-ass was sending messages to others. At school everyone wanted to beat up my friend, but I helped them. I also defended an Arab from Iraq. I just know my rights and want others to respect others.

My Manifesto: Why Hate When You Can Love?

My name is Cristian Dominguez.
Who wants to be poor? Nobody does, it's a "no, no."
Others laugh at the poor people.
Most people tell others that they don't get free or cheap stuff but they do get free education, some get free clothes and free food too.

We are humans who make mistakes by accident. We are not animals or robots. We all make mistakes.

Everyone should go to college or the university to learn how to respect everyone.

We all have to feed and clothe our families and friends. If not we are not showing respect to others.

We are here to be better people, not gang leaders or bad leaders in any kind of way. We are not here to be Hitler's best assistant. We are not here to be a showoff or stupid fake-ass.

We are not here to waste our money on strippers. We are not here for the sex or porn.

We are here to educate our people. We are Native Indians, most of the world is. We do share different cultures in completely different places around the world.

I am a Mexican.
I am an American.
I am a Chicano.
I am a Native Indian.
I am an Asian.
I am a Latino.
I am a North American.
I am a Hispanic.
I am America.

I'm Cristian Dominguez and I'm not perfect, nobody is. I'm not here to waste my time on something bad. I am who I want to be. I will go to college. I will do hard work and will stay at school late until the school closes the door so I can go to college.

I am Cristian Dominguez.

Writing Activity

1. What do you think of Cristian's piece? What stands out to you? How old do you think he is? Do you think age makes you wiser? Do you think youth keeps you creative? Why or why not?

2. Cristian wrote a "manifesto," but he wasn't trying to, he was simply writing what he believes in. Write your own manifesto, or just write what you believe in the same style as Cristian.

   Manifesto: a public declaration of policy and aims, especially one issued before an election by a political party or candidate.

Marlen Gallegos

Marlen Gallegos was born on April 20th, 1998. She was born in Mexico but has been raised in Houston, Texas all her life. She doesn't remember a lot of her hometown but her parents bring the culture with them. Her mom, Maria Guadalupe Monjaras, embraces her Mexican culture by cooking Mexican dishes. Her dad, Joel Gallegos, has also showed his daughter her heritage by making her listen to some of the famous Mexican music styles, such as corridos, norteñas and banda. Marlen is motivated and encouraged by all 6 of her siblings who push her to do her very best as a person and as a scholar. She is the second among all her siblings. She knows that her siblings look up to her as a role model so she does everything to make them proud. She wants to provide a better life than she has had as the child living in a low income sharehold. Marlen has many responsibilities as a teen. She works on the weekends but her priorities lay in her studies. She wants to be in the top five percent of her high school class. She knows that it its going to require work but she is willing to put in the work to get what she wants and to prove to her siblings that anything is possible with determination and hard work. Her big dream is to attend a tier one university. Some of her hobbies include finishing a book series and listening to music. Her favorite genre is k-pop. Her favorite sport is basketball. She is currently pushing herself to do better this 2016 season. She actually won an all-state award for her participation in the JV team. Marlen has many mottos and her personal favorite is living a life without regrets.

What I Wish I Was and What I am

I am a shape shifter that sheds skins from morning to twilight.
Someone that finds an imperfection in anything and is unafraid to show reality.
It is a sin to hide what makes us unique and introvert.
It is a sin and merely a trick in our eyes that allows us to cover the sun with our thumb.
It is a sin that makes all sinners sweat in church.

Do not veil the hideous
Embrace it!
Accept it!
For it is what makes a soul!
Be truth to yourself.

Leave the lies to the politicians and the advertisers
that knock every Saturday morning offering beauty products.
Reject the temptations, say no to the bone of contention
Perhaps sacrifice and carry the cross
Do not be fooled by a reflection or an outcome
Beauty is deadly. Just ask Narcissus
Its misconception can slip and escape like butter.

Let us be free and not limited by an idea or a stereotype
What if?
I am Mexican
What if?
I say troka o chekear
What if?
I eat frijoles y tortillas
Does it mean that I am less than those who eat sushi at Masa in New York starting at $450 before tip?

Let's not discriminate and alienate
Let's call it a truce
History is our role model
Remember the Christmas truce at the Western Front 1914?
Cease fire and "LIVE AND LET OTHERS LIVE"
Stop pulling the trigger on weapons

I am standing on a cliff suspended from a dead tree branch about to fall in a black hole
I don't want to fall
I am afraid I will never see the light of the sky
Help help!!
Ayuda!! Ayuda!! Socorro Socorro!!

Is my call too late?
I don't want to die because someone shoots my way;
I am not bulletproof.
I am a 17 year old aspiring to live past 22.

My lungs are pure. I say no to smoking but that doesn't mean I am immune to cancer.
I want to walk the streets without hearing blurs
that put me down because I am of a dark complexion.

I want to see art but not the one that vandalizes my house.
I want to find love a crush.
I want to experience what it feels to have an unrequited love.
I want to be physical, win a game to shoot and score.
I want the audience to go wild after the ball goes into the basket at the last minute.

Humanity does not need any more genocide like Rwanda's genocides and the Holocaust.
I want to be oxygen, to be accepted by everyone.
I want to be vital for existence.
I want to be a rose in a garden to experience what it feels to belong.

However, I want to be free not anchored in the soil.
I want to be the limit that doesn't exist as X approaches 0.
I don't want my waxed wings to be melted if I get to close to the sun;
I want to keep flying until the Earth collides.
I do not want to drown and suffocate in a pool of mistakes;
I want to swim until I reach the bottom of the ocean
and penetrate through the layers of the Earth.
I want my heart to keep beating to the rhythm of music;
I want to feel the blood stream under my skin.
I don't want my heart to take a break; I want to feel alive.
I want to see all the colors once light bends as it passes air into water.

I want to be at ease with myself. I want others to be clones of Ghandi.
I want to set my ideal every day.
I want to live day by day being an individual being me myself and I.
Days without regrets and what ifs.

A Tangible List

I have a vision of a better tomorrow but I currently only have:
1. A hope stronger than the Wall of China and more stable than the group 18 on the periodic table.
2. A voice and a mind that is more dangerous than the tantrum of a child and more than 1 community begging for change.
    a. A change that will allow everyone to congregate despite religion, race, ethnicity, and age.
    b. A place safe and comforting.
    c. A place without boundaries where parents can be with their children, without the fear to be deported.
    d. A place that allows woman to be equal to men.
    e. A place where money doesn't equal success.
    f. A place that allows low income students to attend college.
    g. A place that feeds the hunger for knowledge of kids the future of tomorrow.
    h. A place people can call home.
    i. A place that gives everyone an opportunity to make their hopes a reality.
    j. A place that dries up the tears of those that cry a river.
    k. A place that doesn't give kids more power if they wear some thing that is of well-known brand.
    l. A place where bystanders do not exist because there is no bullying.
    m. A place that everyone can be a hero or a superstar.
    n. A place that doesn't have funerals at every cemetery.
    o. A place that welcomes life and refuses to destroy embryos.
    p. A place that does not have nuclear weapons of destruction ready to be launched.
    q. A place where my words don't sound foolish, absurd, and childish.
    r. A place that doesn't make my ideas sound cliché and fabricated.
    s. A place that doesn't make me angry at the fact that as I type, as people are dying somewhere in the world.
    t. A place my words can change someone's perspective.
    u. A place that is tangible and not only in my dreams.

To whom it may concern:

There are many summer opportunities out there for everyone's different interests. This 2015, I was introduced to a life changing one. Who knew that a 17-year-old could get published within a week? I cannot wait to share this experience to my classmates once I get back to school. Having said this, I am extremely grateful to have attended Barrio Writers. The Barrio Writers mentors and advisors are one of a kind. Each adviser has a story of their own that connects to everyone in the program. My story starts before I attended the program and how it shaped my way of thinking.

Monday 15 2015

It was around 11:00. I was still in the bed wrapped from head to toe when I was woken up by my sister.
She was silently whispering, "Marlen your friend's mom is here." I quickly woke up shocked as I was like, "is Barrio Writers today?" I had assumed it started Tuesday the 16th. I was like, "oh s**t!" I briskly ran to the restroom and brushed my teeth to greet my friend's mom.
It was awkward walking into the living room in my bright yellow pajama pants but it was necessary to get into my room to change clothes. The night before I had crashed in my mom's bed and I guess she decided not to wake me up. Sike. I probably didn't wake up, forcing her to crash at my bed. I greeted her and saw the smallest opportunity to make a run for my room. I changed at the speed of lightning. I put on a tie dye green shirt that my sister had made. My friend's mom attends the University of Houston where Barrio Writers was hosted so I and my friend didn't have a hard time finding the building.
Once inside, we were required to sign in. We were handled books and immediately we were giving the writing prompt, "why are you here?" As I read the question I was like, "are they being serious here?" In reality, I was just dodging the question because I knew that I couldn't answer the question honestly. Why? Because I didn't know. At first I thought it was because my friend had insisted but then as I was looking around I realized that it was because I desired to improve my writing. After the freewriting, Sarah, one of the founders of Barrio Writers, talked about her experiences and how she beat statistics by getting an education despite her background and being constantly put down by teachers that didn't believe Chicanos were college material.
As I was listening, I was thinking this woman is a fighter. The day ended by

us choosing a prompt. I was eager and scared to write but my pen seemed to know the way. I had a half a page of a poem by the end of the day. Malcom X was a great motivation and the lesson of idioms helped feed my dormant brain. The tutors did an excellent job to start us writing. That was Monday.

Tuesday 16 2015

Classes for Tuesday got cancelled due to Tropical Storm Bill. I was conflicted as I heard the news. One side of me was like, "yes!" but on the other side I was like, "no no no." I was actually looking forward to the lessons. At home I continued to write and as I was typing, trying to ignore my 6 siblings making noise, I realized that as I continued to type the noise seemed distant almost unreal. I had just realized the soothing effect writing had on me. I continued to experiment how the noise changed as I typed at one moment. I can say I reached complete silence. Call me crazy but that's what I felt.

Wednesday 17 2015

My luck wasn't around with me Wednesday. After my friend's mom picked me up, we were not even down the street when she started to smell smoke. My mind went crazy with ideas about what the smell could be. I panicked a little but I kept my calm to show my maturity. Good thing she didn't see my shaky feet. We came into a stop and we saw the smoke coming from the side of the car. I was about to make a run for the door but she was so calm that I also kept my calm. The car had stopped and we were in the middle of the street. AWWW!!! What to do next? She immediately called a friend of hers to come pick us up. Her friend came after some minutes but my dad somehow was passing by and he saw me in the stranded car. My friend's mom kept repeating how embarrassing the whole situation was. After a while I thought it was sort of funny, almost like the start of a cliché movie. He pulled up and tried to help but the car wouldn't start. He helped move the car to the side road and in time, my friend's mom friend picked us up and we were on our way to pick up my friend at school. We arrived at the Barrio Writers on time and we had a lesson out of the ordinary. It was a day where two lessons were combined. It was one of my favorites. I was introduced to the poets Anthony Flores and Chingo Bling. They are the best. 'Huevo Rancheros' by Flores had my head rolling. It was so interesting to see how someone can choose a dish of their culture and give it so many meanings. I emulated his writing style later in my free writing. I choose quesadillas con chile:

Quesadillas con chile are the new sweet bread they can be grilled or toast.
Quesadillas con chile is what I eat.
Quesadillas con chile are what mothers give to show their love.

Thursday 18 2015

Thursday I was excited and eager to attend Barrio Writers. Through the week I had started talking to other participants so I didn't feel like a fish out of the water. Thursday was my favorite day. The lessons were on point. All the writers introduced to us were musicians as well. I was like man this is cool. Not only are they authors but they use their words as their strongest weapon as Sarah would say. We ended the day attending the Station Museum to see the exhibit. The pieces of art were out of this world. For example, Wayne Gilbert actually created his portraits out of human remains, the ashes. As a peer said it must have taken guts. The portraits were live and full of color. My eyes went wild. I knew that I had to write about this. My head was spinning with thoughts. That was not only it but there was an exhibit called 'Sin Huellas,' a room-like scenario of what people are experiencing in immigration detention centers. The room gave me goosebumps. It was cold and had no life. I felt useless and ignorant as I saw the letters of those calling out for help. I wanted to help them, to pull them out of their misery and pain but I was just standing in the room looking at the bodies. However, I realized that the best way to help them now is to draw more attention to their situation and hardships. That is why I decided to dedicate my words to them. I want to help those in the detention center. I want to use my words as their weapon to fight this war. Houstonians, this problem is not distant from us. Let's open our eyes and acknowledge this situation. I was blind to it but I am aware and willing to help. Let's join the immigrant activists in Houston. Let's unite our voice to create change. They need our help. How can one sleep at night when many have been separated from families and deported back? I don't want to remain silent to the injustices and I don't want to be fool like I was before Thursday. I don't want my days to go by without helping someone, even if it just means opening the door for someone. THANK YOU!!! Barrio Writers for helping me find a purpose in life .The obstacles I faced this week are insignificant to the real situations that should be addressed.

Sincerely,
MG

Untitled

I am strong. I am loud.
I am a megaphone with everlasting battery
My voice is the voice of generations
Of ancient preachers.
I speak for those that have their tongues
tied up.
My voice is loud and clear
That makes the ground tremble and windows shatter
as I speak for equality.
Liars and thieves run away
as I open my mouth.
It is unbearable sometimes to
have this voice of mine.
The only people that seem to like
me are borrachos and kids.
Other women escape my
voice or hide in their houses and refuse
to listen to me.
They rather prefer to die and burn
at the stakes
then to open their ears and let
tmy voice flow through
ignorant women.
I just want to help them.
I want wives and muchachas
to go to school and be educated and
to not be dependent on a man.
 I want my voice to speak
equality but the doors close on me.
Could it be that my voice
And call for justice is threading
I don't want to scare anyone but
I am willing to put up a fight
with my voice to gain what I
Envision
I am not going to back down because I was taught to
Always speak my mind.
By a women that was marginalized by machistas

By thoughts that accused her of being a mujer de la calle
I want women to
Show off their curves
And not to be discriminated
I have a voice as a member of the multiple communities
And I will use my weapon and its mind
to fight the Barriers.
My voice is silent as a knight
but as lethal as an arrow that can tear even the crustiest heart.
My voice is the new atlas that will hold the feminist world of tomorrow.

Writing Activity

1. Marlen uses several words/phrases that aren't 'real words' or 'correct,' such as shareheld, chekear, and find love, yet they work for her art and beyond. What are some words that you've used that aren't 'correct' or 'real?' Who says they aren't? Try and come up with at least 3 of those words. Write a poem where you use all those words that responds to those say they aren't 'real' or 'correct.'

2. What is the 'hideous' part of you? Why is it 'hideous?' This may be an adjective (a word used to describe you, like ugly or dumb) or a noun (a word used to define you, like thug.) Does it define you? Write a poem where you explore this 'hideous' part of you and how it isn't true, how it is a strength. You may find that these words have no power over you. Also, remember that you don't have to share this with anyone.

3. Marlen wrote a poem using litany (a list) saying everything she wants to see come true. What's your list? What do you want to see in the world?

    a. If you agree with Marlen, respond to her poem by adding to her list with details. For Example, "A place that allows woman to be equal to men." What does that look like to you? Or why does this poem need to say this?"

Diana Angelica De La Riva

Diana Angelica De La Riva was born on August 2, 2001 and raised in Nacogdoches, Texas. She is the youngest of Juan and Elvia De La Riva's three children. She loves to read, draw, and write. She is currently a freshman at Nacogdoches High School. Her dreams consist of attending college and eventually becoming an author or a teacher. Her biggest influences are her family and best friend, Magdalena Davalos.

"Testify"

"Now testify…It's right outside our door"
—Rage Against The Machine

Many of us see many things going on in the world that are problems, but most of us keep quiet about it. We see it all the time, through a book, a movie, or even "right outside our door", but no one wants to say something to someone else because they have a "reason" not to or they are just scared maybe even feel threatened. You hear about it all the time everywhere, so why not stop it? Rape, child abuse, assault, attempted murder, these words seem familiar right?

They do, and that is a problem, some people shouldn't have to worry about these things going on! We hear about these things but no one dares say much, if anything. People think others are trying to stop it, so they don't say anything about it, or some lie so they don't have to say anything about it. It's all over the media and it keeps getting worse, so if people are putting an end to it, why is it getting worse?

Like in the quote from the song 'Testify" by Rage Against the Machine, we have to "testify" these things are going on because they keep happening "right outside our door."

Though this may not have happened to you, it still involves you because it is still going on. But if you haven't noticed you are genuinely oblivious or trying to be.

Writing Activity

1. Do you know Rage Against The Machine's music? Listen to "Testify" (you can find it online), then reread Diana's piece. How was she inspired by the lyrics?

2. Is there a song that inspires you? (If not, use "Testify.") Listen to it, write your response to it. Then share it, read it out loud with the music playing in the background!

> In a **response piece**, you analyze the writing (in this case the song), but you also include your personal impression. Sometimes it's just something the writing made you think about, a small connection to the words, images and theme.

Adamaris Ramirez

My name is Adamaris Ramirez and I was born in Garden Grove, California on August 29th. I am the youngest out of three children. I live with my sister, Tzitzitlin, and her husband, Ramon, in downtown Santa Ana. My greatest inspiration is my sister because she supports me with every decision I make. Every sport I played she was there on the sidelines cheering me on. Growing up I was an introvert, my sister and her husband would make me write poems and recite it in front of them. Writing poems helped me step out of my comfort zone and become more social. My mom, Enriqueta, always told me to be a chingona in everything I do. My mom is a beautiful hard working woman who works just so my sister, brother and I could have a future. My mom is the most important person to me, without her I don't think I would be able to survive. In ten years I would like to see myself attend a University in San Diego or Berkley, studying to be a sports therapist. I believe that I can achieve my goal and be the first person in my family to graduate from a University with the support of my loved ones.

Dia de Los Muertos

Painted Faces
Marigolds surrounding loved ones
Every alter with its own story to tell
Candles burning

Papel picado everywhere
Chinelos dancing getting everybody hyped
This day isn't just an ordinary day
We all get to spend the day with our loved ones that have left us
Dia de los Muertos expresses the way we feel through creating an alter.

Writing Activity
1. Dia de Los Muertos/Day of the Dead is celebrated throughout Mexico, in particular the Central and South regions, and by people of Mexican ancestry living in other places, especially in the United States. Is there a cultural tradition you take part in?

2. What kind of significance does your cultural or family tradition have on you? Discuss the importance with your group in ways that a tradition is important to have with loved ones.

3. Next time you attend a Dia de Los Muertos/Day of the Dead event in your area, ask altar makers what is their story behind the altar, and describe the different types of items without giving the name of it in any writing form you want.

Graciella Castillo

Graciella Castillo, better known by the nickname "Lala," was born in San Antonio, Texas on April 3, 1998. She then moved to Austin, Texas shortly after. She is going to be a senior and has hopes of graduating and continuing on to attend college.

Is She Mexican?

She has dark skin, dark eyes,
and even darker hair.
I assume she speaks Spanish.
She is probably from Mexico
I will call her Mexican.

In what little Spanish I know,
I say, "Hola, como estas?"
She doesn't understand.

I ask her, this time in English,
if she knows what Mexico is like.
She doesn't have a clue.

No Mexico?
No Spanish?
Not even an accent?
Is she Mexican?

I learn that we listen to the same music
and wear the same clothes.
We are from the same country
and speak the same language.
There is no way she is Mexican.

I will call her white.

Writing Activity

1. Have you ever felt as though someone makes assumptions about you based on the way you look, the way you talk or act? Write a scene about a time that has happened to you and how it made you feel.

2. When people rely on stereotypes to try to understand a person or their culture, what happens to that person's identity? What can we do when we face those "stereotype threats"? Make a list of negative stereotypes that society attributes to your culture/race/religion, etc. and then on the other side of the paper, make a list that counters those stereotypes with positive examples that empower you.

3. In this poem, Graciella wrote from the point of view of someone who makes hurtful assumptions about the girl based on their ignorance. It can be difficult to use the voice of someone we are angry with in our writing, but sometimes it helps us to understand the point of view of those people in order to heal ourselves. Write a persona poem using the voice of someone that makes you angry or upset, and explore where you think their actions or thoughts come from.

Anonymous Barrio Writer

This Barrio Writer chose to remain anonymous for reasons they wish to not state. We hope you enjoy their writing.

Living in a Zoo

I'll be better than this, this time. The only problem is I won't. I can't be better than who I am because who I am and who I will always be is the fucked up version of what you want me to be. What you want me to be would've stayed in the house and taken your crap. I'll be better than this, this time but me, being not what you want me to be, made the impulsive decision to leave. I just had to get you out of my head. I had to. I'd say sorry but I'm not. If I kept you in my head, I would've wound up dead. Now that doesn't sound that the fairytale ending you say you hope for me. But I'm telling you now, it will never happen again. I'll be better than this, this time. You think my every word, a lie. Might as well make that truth a lie.

Hyperventilating as I run now. I am fast but my heart is heavy. It's slowing me down. Flashing lights start to catch up to me. I fought the strong men hard but they were convinced that I would be better off dying in my dear old house than on the streets of today.

Ok, I know it's happened multiple times now but I'm changing. I'll be better than this, this time. Pardon me for yelling but you're under my skin again. These people, these lions, they are always here. They're trying to eat me, blood running down their chin. I know that I can fight them, but I don't want to let them in. This sacred room of mine was all I had but they have taken control. Oh looked, I lied. Here I am, running, running faster than before. My heavy heart is sinking, heavier than before. I'm fighting the strong men, stronger than before. Well it looks like I'm the animal now I guess, bars on the window. You know, in the backseat cage. That's funny. The lions were trying to eat me, now it feels like I'm one of them. But look at them! They aren't caged! They are free. That's how they got to me the first time. They live with me.

Centuries later, I am out of the cage to get some sunlight. This time will be different. I'll change for real. Go on. Say it! If you say it enough, you might actually start believing it. I'll be better than this, this time. I promise guys. Oh promises, promises! Do I keep them? It's not like I don't try. What's left of my sanity tries. It leaves a lie. She calls it hope. That lie only lasts for so long before the lions attack again and I'm left without a choice. The un-caged beasts attack me. Running again now. The flashing lights are relentless. Figures in uniform cut of the circulation in my hands. Wrists behind my back, I'm thrown back into the cage. Well, back to the zoo.

Writing Activity

1. Have you ever wished you could write or speak about something without people criticizing you for it? Almost as if you were anonymous to them? What are the advantages to speaking/writing anonymously? What are the disadvantages?

2. Read the piece by "Anonymous." Discuss why this Barrio Writer may have chosen to remain anonymous. Although the story uses elements of a "fable" and "magical realism," it still speaks to a real life feeling. In your own words, what do you think the author was really talking about?

4. What "pen name" would you choose for yourself? Choose one. Then write a story or personal opinion under your pen name. Share it or post it publically without disclosing that you're the author. Then wait for the unbiased reactions or dismiss them and just enjoy sharing your ideas openly. ☺

> **Pen Name:** an assumed name used by a writer instead of their real name.

Alyssa Richards

My name is Alyssa Richards. Born June 4, 2002, I was a healthy seven-pound baby with my whole life ahead of me, but around the age of eight that slowly faded away. That was the year my parents separated. I took it pretty hard but I'm not the type to really show my true emotions so I kept it all inside. Then I got to the point where I couldn't take it anymore and instead of telling someone, I started writing. Short stories, poems, a few rants every now and then. And that's when I found my voice, in between those blue lines, and I joined Barrio Writers to further develop that voice.

CRUSH

i can't concentrate when You're around .
i feel like i'm floating ten feet off the ground, and can't come down.
But really, i don't even want to land, really don't think i can.
i just want You to hold my hand.
You're all i think about in homeroom.
i dream of lunch. Can noon come soon?
i'm living with a little pain, every minute i'm losing an ounce of my self gain.
You don't even know my name!
After You read this will You look at me the same?
Will our relationship always be just a silly little game?
If so I can no longer play...
But will you stay?

Writing Activity

1. Read Alyssa's poem out loud as a group, then take time to look at each line. What do you notice about her choice in style? How does she change the style in the poem towards the end? Why do you think she changed it like that?

   Style: a manner of doing something, a distinctive appearance (like fashion in clothes), or to design or make in a particular form.

2. Have you ever had a crush? (Don't lie, we have all had at least one.) Without stating their name, write about how you felt around your "crush." When did you realize you were putting them first and forgetting about yourself? How did you get over your crush? Or maybe it wasn't crush, maybe it was a real relationship. Either way, write about it and learn about yourself in the process.

Noemi Ocampo

Noemi Ocampo was born on November 2, 2002 in Santa Ana, California. She's 12 and attends Doig Intermediate School. She lives with her father, mother, and younger brother. They may not be the perfect family but they know they will always be there for each other. During her free time she likes to read a book which is called "Story of a Girl," which was recommended by one of her teachers. She also likes to watch Netflix 24/7. Noemi joined Barrio Writers because one of her cousins recommended it to her. At first, she thought she wasn't going to like it but once she got there she started to like it. Barrio Writers helped her express her own words. Noemi's parents always get phone calls from school, she doesn't follow the rules, never pays attention, and she's well, a troublemaker. Her teachers are very strict with her because they all believe in her, even though she gives all of them a hard time. She dreams of attending one of her ideal universities: Arizona State University, NYU, or Columbia University. Her dream career is to help immigrants and become a lawyer.

Society

Many people are afraid of expressing themselves because of society
People judge other people because of their appearance
How they dress

Who their peers are
and their race
We are all human
We all have a different style
What makes anyone different?
Everyone dresses up
Everyone has a face
Everyone has peers, don't you?
Everyone has a type of race
People express themselves the way you do
Everyone has their own styles
Society is supposed to be safe
It's not

Writing Activity

1. Why do people immigrate to America? Do you believe children should be punished for arriving to United States without permission? Why do you think your family immigrated to the U.S.?

2. Have you ever been bullied? If so how did it make you feel? Like Noemi, write a poem that questions those who have made you feel bullied or less than, express yourself freely.

Matthew Lopez

I was born in Houston Texas on June 10, 1997. Raised by my grandparents, my single mother was always working. But even through the drama, I still appreciated everything she did for me. I mean somehow, bills had to get paid. But for me it wasn't about money. Writing rhymes was my only escape. Still dropped out at 13, couldn't take no more disappointment and discrimination. I had dreams of being the first in my immediate family to see graduation day. Walk the stage and feel the praise, but once poverty struck us, I felt I was to blame and I was Alone and didn't have enough strength to make it through another day of high school.

Thankfully…I found HOPE. Faith in god through blessings of mysterious ways.

Now 18, finally back in school and Succeeding and Turning DREAMS to REALITY.

My Big Brother

My big brother helped me discover
Lifes mo than purchasing boats sailing coast to coast, while wearing coats made of chinchilla.

I had to perceive life thru my eyes and discover,

Being the best MC is not defined by Best selling CDz, being on dat DISCCOVER.

Yeah, that shit feels great when you can make yo mom's best day, sail yo boat on yo lake,
Pay all the bills n still have mo dough to take…

YO FAM away from oppression, I'd need 20 tickets to outta space.
Lifes mo than blowing them candles n cake…

Make a wish B4 you lose Faith ,it's too late in my hood, THEY have NO FAITH, it's gone
Walking thru my hood at night my souls the only street light on…

Bring yo kidz inside b4 them AKz start fishing for men's pride.
we alive, but we living thru the new Draft and prohibition…

We "poe cause our men and women" are drivin by false ambitions.

There will always be mo niggas and bitches " poe and bitchin" ..
OPEN yo eyes and ears, when I'm speaking and feel that your sensational children…don't jus listen.

We're Alive but we live in Country and state of Capitalism -RULES like we back on the plantation.

FOOLZ OPEN yo eyes, CHANGE!

Our Culture, Country and STATE of mind! STRIVE to be better than yo MOM and BIG BROTHA!!

My Male Role Model

Why are athletes and rappers my Rappers my Role modelz?
Prolly Cuz I Never met my biological Father ..
NO FATHER "Figures"

Another Adolescent minority with NO FATHER FIGURES
NO ROLE MODELZ!

Jus my niggas who showed me how to Swang Candy Impalas
Roll Bluntz don't put .. Dank so you wont go home Stankn
Poe up Drank . Sip slow Bro, don't leave stainz , N try to Break the Bank!
Filln Dat Bitch with Cash
Strive to it legal N give back to our people.

STAND UP FIGHT BACK!

When were treated unequal.
Love ones die bein caught CrossFire.
I Roll 2 Bluntz 4 Onez datz gone to the Next life
What I call the Sequel ...

All my Mentors 6 feet under
First Off R.I.P. Uncle Phil
Taught me how to be a real man Treat my Wife, Kids , Legally Pay Billz
But that's a T.V. show
When its ova im back In Reality

With Sirens as my Alarms
GHETTO BIRDS My Pets
CHOPPAZ My Wind Chimes

My perceptionz stained

Ironically
The ONLY Stable Family I know is on Cable T.V.
FALSE IMADGRY

Shit! Is dat the good life?
Jus look at all the opportunities

They have Both Parents !!
With PHDz Black history, Masters in Law and you got a black butler named Jeffrey
Foldin Clothes, Changin Diapers , Cookin meals Cleaning .
Everything in between...

Can YOU See?? Irony...

My Perception Stained!
On my block I was taught to seek scrilla Not Dreams.

Tough Love what I Got .
Till I seen uncle phil
Taught me how to be a Popz N what bein a Father N Role Model meanz .

The Only REAL Fathers Real MEN I heard from or seen were in Bookz, Rhymes on Cdz, T.V sceenz.

My Perception Stained…

How should we Treat our
Women n children
Elders n Siblingz

Even Peerz NAuthority
Law Enforcement made me Burst into Tears
When my brother was in chainz Facin Years.

SHIT. Dats Real Life!

We all jus tryna make a Dolla Bill Right??

Cuz who Pays billz, buyz Meal, sets Examples N Makes Rules.

But when you're a Rebelous Teenager you Say
"FUCK RULES I SET MY OWN EXAMPLES"

While thru perifieles lookin up to the KING OF CAMPUS.
With his picture perfect family, got all the money, live in a Mansion
Rockin Fanciest Clothes. Drivin Newest Cars, Ridn with Badest hoes.

Why?

Prollly Cuz I was less fortunate.
Idolized materialistic thingz that seem to bring partial happiness n Importance.
Atleast for a split second.

Like I said my PERCEPTIONZ STAINED.

Where im from there hardly Any Prep. Skoolz that let
Less fortunate youth In.

Goin to college thru scholarships had a completely different meanin

Shit you can be a dumbass
Fail all test in class
TEACHER STILL PASS

Why tired of lack of attention in class or lack of winning our skool team has.

He or she still blessed with God Givin Ability Amazing Body N Capability
To be the Mos Outstanding Athlete

That aint gunna get you but so far, plan to graduate college have a career
NOT LEGIT JOBZ

Butcha still gotta have a clean RAP SHEET N MY SHIT DIRTY

Wrote so many Lyricz Changed perspectives
Call me Makaveli

RE RE RE Reincarnated

My mindz still tainted
Perceptionz Stained

Cause im from a hood Deprived, Foreign to thingz
Such As stable Enviromentz, Picture Perfect Families

I know a couple thingz MONEY cant buy
Happiness, love, strong faith, Hope for better Dayz

I know First, Second
On the Third Hand im a Hard Working Determind young Man
I know when you work for something and succeed
THAT FEELINZ Parellel
To heaven 4 Me

I feel grown and I feel I have so much to grow

Finally made it finally Famous!
Yet still Unknown!
Yeah I took the Long road but it paid off.

Whateva didn't kill my Soul
Made me stronger
Now I can go back to My Hood
In The WORST Clothes, No Car, No Hoes
ONE DEEP IN JAIL ROUTE

Feel the love, pain, Strength and appreciation
being BROKE BRINGZ

Do you still ask why the homeless and less fortunate have the
MOS Faith, Happiness

We have been without all our lives
We know all you Truly Need is
Gods embrace Loving Words
Turned to Thoughts

OUR FATHER
MY TRUE FATHER
RAISED A T.H.U.G.

A TRUE HERO UNDER GOD.

Writing Activity

1. What decisions have you had to make that you didn't like and/or agree with? Why did you make that decision? How has it affected you? Write a story of how you came to make that decision.

2. What do you find hope in? How does it drive you in what you do? Where does that hope take you? Write a poem dedicated to that hope.

3. Matthew wrote his pieces in hip hop form. It is poetry in its own right that comes from a different history and heritage in America, making it a distinctly American art form. Give hip hop a try. Start by writing a poem with words that rhyme, like the form: AA, BB, CC,

etc. For example: Like & bike, choke & joke, family & destiny. You'll find that these words have connections, you just have to make these connections.

Kaiden Brown

Kaiden Brown, 15, is a young writer that one day, after joining the Air Force, hopes to become a famous writer and pursue their dream of entertaining others.

Different

Do you know that
Feeling?
The feeling of cold hands,
Pushing you away
Deeper
Deeper into the
Darkness
Those faces
They laugh
They taunt
They haunt
Your every dream
Every nightmare
Why?
You scream in
Agony
Why me?
"Because" a voice

Whispers
So close
So cold
In your ear
"You're different"
You close your
Eyes
And take a deep
Breath
Standing
You pull away from
The hands
"What's so
Different about
Me?
Every second
We all
Breathe
We all
Fight
Just to see who's
Right.
How are you and
I so
Different?
You don't breathe or
See what
Equality means to
Be?
Open your eyes
For a
Surprise.
We're all the
Same
You see,
You
And
Me.

Writing Activity

1. In their poem, Kaiden focuses on being "different," have you ever felt like you were the one who is different—at school, in your neighborhood or in your family? What emotion did you experience because you were "different"? Do you think being different is a good or bad thing? How can it be the opposite feeling?

2. Reread Kaiden's bio. They identify with the term "their" versus his or her. What does that mean? What does gender non-conforming mean? Does that mean Kaiden is different? Should they be considered "different" or human?

3. Write your own bio in third person **without** using gender specific pronouns (she, he, her, him, his, hers). Write about your life, any challenges you may have overcome as well as your accomplishments.

   Writing your bio is good practice, it will help you feel comfortable writing about yourself when you have to complete college, scholarship and job applications.

   Afterwards, read your bio aloud, does it matter that you used gender neutral pronouns, does it mean you're "different"?

Rosalinda Segura

My name is Rosalinda Segura. I am 16 years old and currently attend Santa Ana Valley High School. I was born on April 28th as the youngest of my family. I am a shy and serious girl but if you stick around long enough you get to see how weird I am. I am always there for the people I care about and I tend to help them more than myself. The one thing that keeps me going is music. It has saved my life a million times when I didn't want to continue living. Music is a gate way to everything I love to do. I love to sing, dance, write, read, draw and well almost everything that has to do with ARTs I love. I had to grow up very fast due to the problems that were thrown to me at a young age. Also due to me growing up so fast I've been trying to fit into people's expectations and well…that wasn't so good for me. I've given up on life so many times I actually can't count on my fingers due to the fact that I thought I failed so many people. After actually finding out who I am—really am—which I'm still discovering everyday, through music, my friends and some of my family. I could care less about people's expectations that I have to "fit in." One of the many reasons I came into this program is not just to make my mom and friends proud, it's to make myself proud that I'm actually doing something I love. Also to express myself into my writing and try to make a connection with the reader to maybe make them see that they aren't alone.

Woman

The definition of "woman" is different for you and I
You think, I should serve a man everything and do everything for a man
You think, I should not have friends that are guys or else we are "having sex"
I should show my skin but not so much or else I'm a whore
I have to have my education but only up to high school or else I'm emasculating a man and I'm not suppose to do that.
I have to look my best 24/7
I have to marry a man and let him take care of me for the rest of my life
Wanna know what I have to say about your expectation?

FUCK THEM!
You can get up and serve yourself sometimes
I am NOT your maid
I am NOT going to do everything for you
I have guy friends!
And you know what?
We haven't had sex because they respect me and I don't see them that way
They are my best friends and I WILL NOT give them up because YOU want me to
Yeah I wear shorts, skirts, and tank tops
but I am not going to let a man
touch my ass or my boobs because of that
I will go to a university
because I want to do great things in my life
If a man feels emasculated because of that?
I don't give a fuck!
I will do what I love to do and be the best at it!
I am capable of taking care of myself
I don't need saving
I am a strong, independent woman!
Just because I am a woman
doesn't mean you have to treat me as a fragile object
that you can push around
I am human just like YOU
Start treating me and respecting me like one.

Different Yet So Alike

She loves to sing but he loves to dance
She loves rock music but he prefers dub-step
She was more of an introvert and him, an extrovert
They were different but somehow liked each other
She loved to explain her passions and show people how awesome they are but also loves to hear and see how/what motivates others
He was more into his and didn't share and didn't hear other people's
She loved old fashion things like 1965 mustangs and the 50's dance and fashion
He couldn't wait for the new fashion trends

Even though they were different they somehow fell for each other
Then they found out they were a little a like

They both love anime
They would love to explore different cities
They find their friends more as family than their actual family
They both want to inspire people, to keep on going, to follow their dreams
How the one thing that helps the, keep on going is their music
Even Though they are very different they are also very alike

My Place in Santa Ana

I get to see him there even though he isn't physically there
I speak to the ground and he responds by the sound of the wind
I feel his presence
feel his hand on my shoulder
calming me down
as I stroke the grass above where he lays
I smell his cologne once I step off the car with a bunch of red roses
I can let out all of my thoughts there
telling him how much I miss him
how I've been doing
I get to hear how proud he is of me
for going on with my life,
chasing my dreams
becoming the great young lady that I am

I hear him thanking me
for being there for him
even though I had other things I had to do
thanking me
for taking care of my mom,
aunts, uncles and my grandmother while he is gone

My favorite place is my grandfather's tomb
because he means everything to me

Writing Activity
1. Given the definitions below, how would you describe a hero, shero and superhero? Refer to physical and personality traits. Who is your hero, shero, and favorite superhero and why?

    hero: a person, typically a man, who is admired or idealized for courage, outstanding achievements, or noble qualities.

    shero: a women regarded as a hero.

    superhero: a benevolent fictional character with superhuman powers, such as Superman.

5. Who are the women in your life that inspire you? Research these women whom have been questioned because they use their voice to express how they feel about politics and society.
    a. Angela Davis
    b. Assata Shakur
    c. Jennicet Gutierrez
    d. Katherine Figueroa

Miakoda Earley

Miakoda Earley is a 16-year-old high school student living with her mom, dad, grandpa, and two younger sisters in Round Rock, Texas. She is the Co-Captain of Texas Junior Roller Derby in Austin. She's accompanied by the constant presence of anxiety and depression, but pushes through with the help of her boyfriend and family. She aspires to enroll in art school as soon as she graduates.

Dec. 2013
So I'm a fourteen-year-old girl, short, shy, awkward, quiet, and this boy says to me, "You're beautiful, will you be my girlfriend?" Alright now you know the sound of TV static? That's what my head felt like. So we're at this roller skating rink and he's wearing this gory band shirt, black swooshy emo hair... and I said yes.

Feb. 2014
Things are going well, I got a boyfriend, had my first kiss, my friends hate him, I'm on fire! I can't talk to him. If I have a bad day or if I have the audacity to feel sad, he's guaranteed to have something worse. But that's okay, I'm his girlfriend. I'm supposed to be there for him. I'm fine.

Mar. 2014
He asks for something...I'm his girlfriend, I'm supposed to want this, I'm

supposed to make him happy right? I said yes. I'm fine.

Mar. 2014
He asks for something, I really don't want to, but I can't disappoint him, I'm supposed to want it, I can't risk him leaving, right? So the words "I don't know" carefully escaped my lips. I guess "I don't know" was close enough to "yes" for him. I'm fine.

April 2014
He asks me if I want to go farther…What the hell?! I'm fifteen! NO! No, no, no. He tells me, he promises me…"Whenever you're ready."

April 2014
He asks me again. "No." His sad helpless, pitiful look tells me I've disappointed him. "No." Well shit, I'm not being a good girlfriend, so I changed my answer.

May 2014
I'm fine, everything's fine.

Writing Activity

1. Miakoda wrote a diary entry in response to the young adult novel *Gabi, a Girl in Pieces* by Isabel Quintero. In this book, Gabi, the protagonist, shares a year in her life during her senior year in high school when everything seems like it's falling apart. Consider how this writer uses diary entries to track her character's feelings about a relationship over time. How can diaries help us examine and make sense of events in our lives, especially events we avoid talking about? Even in diary form, which is supposed to be emotionally open, we sometimes limit ourselves to what we are willing to tell. Think about an event in your life that was difficult to share with others, or even difficult for you to understand at the time. Write a diary entry or multiple entries about this event and track how your perception of it changes over several entries.

2. Often times, writers will use repetition to emphasize something. Miakoda uses the repetition of the phrase "I'm fine" throughout her piece. What does this repetition communicate about the trauma the character has faced? Think of a phrase you use when people ask if you're alright, even when you're not. Use it to write your own poem or prose piece.

3. Think about a time in which someone asked you to do something that made you uncomfortable or that you weren't ready for. How did that make you feel? What was your response then? How would you respond to them now? Write how you felt and how you responded then, and then write a letter or response to that person now, and compare how the two. This can be a safe way to explore a difficult event.

Jennifer Belen Alvarez

Jennifer Belen Alvarez was born on July 1st, 1997 in Santa Ana, California. When she was one year old, her mother took her and her sisters, Abigail and Perla to Mexico. There she lived with her Mama, Abuelitos, Tios, Tias, and many, many Primos y Primas. She had a blissful childhood filled with happy memories and raised for five years with love from all those around her. Unfortunately, like a fairytale, her life drastically changed for the worst. She returned to Santa Ana at six years of age. She struggled to adjust to a new country and language. Fortunately, in fourth grade she discovered her passion for writing thanks to her teacher Mrs. Hanks whom she admires and respects so much. During this time her family welcomed a baby boy, David, and the family expanded. She hopes to attend a private four-year university and continue to write about her life. She hopes for a bright future filled with blissful happiness.

People

Why kill?
People kill, it's something everyone knows
But do people have the right to kill?
Of course not, no one has that right
Then why?

I'll tell you why
Fear
Hate
Revenge
Oppression
Evil
But it all boils down to the lack of
Empathy
Humanity
Respect
Connection
And most importantly,
Love for Life

Policing for Dummies

Step 1: In order to avoid controversies revolving racial discrimination stop judging people based on their race and color. Stop discrimination!

Step 2: Stop derogating any certain group. This can be done by AVOIDING STEOTYPES or just accepting anyone different from you.

Step 3: Don't shoot to kill! Shoot to immobilize the aggressor by aiming your gun at the various extremities, not the heart or head, or maybe, to be more effective, avoid using your gun altogether.

As a cop, these rules should be engraved in your brain. Just as you are trained to shoot, why aren't you trained to empathize with people and show humanity and mercy?

Why aren't you?

All that training you went through didn't teach you empathy did it? It didn't teach you to be HUMANE huh?

Why not?
A killer is not a hero
A police is a protector of peace
Killing and murdering, does not bring peace
It brings hate, revenge, rage,

But not peace
DO YOUR JOB RIGHT!!!!

Sincerely,
Those who have been and felt victimized:
Husbands,
Wives,
Mothers,
Fathers,
Children,
Teens,
Teens in Hoodies,
Grandmothers,
Uncles,
Aunts
Cousins,
Basically all Humanity
Get the point?

I am me

To the world,
I am a Mexican-American
Whose probability of graduating and going into a four year university are low

To myself,
I am a Mexican- American that will graduate high school and enter a private university
I have defied the odds
I will continue to defy them
For I have become the odds
I abhor the idea of fitting into a mold that constricts me into only one thing
I am forever changing always reinventing myself
I am undefeatable, indescribable
I am me
A person without a definition
A person always morphing into something new
A person that lacks a definition because it's limiting
Definitions do not leave room for progress or change

And what is the purpose of life without change?
Is it even a life?
Trees grow and wither away
The sun rises and sets
It is change
I am change
I am not done
I won't be done for a very long time
Maybe when I'm in my deathbed, funeral or what not
Then, someone will try to define me, but will they?
No, they won't
They won't wrap my entire life into a few sentences
It will be impossible
I'll make it impossible
For I am me

Writing Activity

1. Write your own writing guide piece like Jennifer's "Policing for Dummies". Direct your writing guide piece towards in response to when you and your family have been oppressed.

   Oppression: unjust treatment, mental pressure or control.

2. Jennifer is an empowering young woman who is active in her community. How does your identity shape your goals? Write a letter to all the goals you want to accomplish and why is it important to you?

Gabriella Isget

Gabriella Isget is 16 years old and she comes from a long extensive family of bold Hispanic women and men. Her rich Hispanic American culture has sculpted her to be the person she is today. She found a love for writing and art at a young age and hasn't looked back since.

Empty Box

I want to change the way I am seen.
I want to change the way my people are seen.
I don't want to be seen by my color.
I don't want to be seen by my color.
I don't want to be seen by my brown hair.
I don't want to be seen by my brown eyes.

I want to change; I want to eliminate the image of a Mexican, Hispanic, Chicana, Chicano person. I want to see people classifying humans, as they want to be seen.

Border jumper.
Mexican.
Dark.
Bad English.
Big lips.

Big butt.
Dark eyes.
Black hair.
Thick thighs.
Curly hair.
Spicy.
Housewife.
Labor.
Illegal.
Welfare.
Ghetto.

I would change the way mixed people have to classify themselves. Either or, no both.

There is no box that says multiracial; there is no box that says mixed.

I am mixed.
I am multicultural.
I am multiracial.
I am Hispanic.
I am Caucasian.

But I can never be both. Either or. People see me as only Mexican , so there fore that is what I MUST classify myself as. I am no longer mixed. I am no longer Caucasian…
I classify myself as white I am no longer Mexican. Now I am just "confused" they say.
"But you look MEXICAN"
I hate that comment.
Not that I hate my image, not that I hate that I look Mexican but that my image can only put me in ONE category.

I don't want these stereotypes weighed down on my people. We shouldn't have to explain "how we got to the states" when we were born here! We shouldn't have to explain to the unfamiliar aye that I a woman am striving for a career.
We shouldn't have to explain to the unfamiliar eye that I attend college unlike the "common Mexican female."

I don't want to explain to the world that I shouldn't be seen or treated any less because of others stereotypes I resemble!
I am confused.
The pale skin blue eyed person asks me why I stumble on some words.
The Hispanic asks me why I don't speak fluent Spanish.

I am never American ENOUGH.
I am never Mexican ENOUGH.
I am TOOO American.
I am TOOO Mexican.
I am TOOO me.

You Know It

I got my eyes on you
I see you walking my way
Your pride in your eyes
Your heart on your sleeve
There is no turning back
You've captured me with one look

This was our moment.

Heavy Eyes

I feel it coming
I feel it growing
I hear his laugh
Short
Deep
I feel him entering
I feel the burning
I a no longer home
I am six again
It is no longer it it is now a he
He
This man I know, I knew
My grandfather

Dead, Gone, Irrelevant
But he is back
Back in my head
Back in my soul "Hello again" he whispers
I am no longer home
I am six again
The smell of harsh smoke
The sound of screams
The light from the fire
I see the RED,
The red symbol drawn on my floor
I am no longer home
I am six again
My eyes shut
My arms open
Searching blindlessly for me
For my home.
I am no longer home.
I am six again.
"Hello again" his whisper engulfs me

His remains

I can feel the pain in my grandma's eyes
I can see her loneliness
She does not speak of it
Never
She does not say "Mija I just want to be loved"
I see her hands ball up when she passes the couple on the street
I see the fire in one eye and a tear in the other.
I can see her heart shattered up and down the sleeves of her shirt
She doesn't know.
She doesn't know I see it.
We climb into bed and she tells me to pray.
I pray for a smile to appear on her face
I pray for the knife in her back to disappear.
I say Amen and I hear her mumbling something in Spanish I cant understand.
I scoot closer to where I can feel her harsh fast breathing through her back.
I hug her. Longer, tighter, than ever before.
I never noticed the fears you could feel on a persons back.

Writing Activity

1. What is the difference between the terms "Hispanic," "Mexican-American," and "Chicano"? Why do some people use "Chican@" and others "Chicanx"?

2. Create a list of all your identities (race, ethnicity, religion, gender), even subcultures if you identify with them. How do you identify or fit into those identities, are there some you hide from family and/or friends? Why or why not?

   Subcultures are values and norms distinct from those of the majority and are held by a group within a wider society. In the United States, subcultures might include hippies, Goths, fans of hip hop or heavy metal and even bikers - the examples are endless.

3. Like Gabriella, write a piece that incorporates who you and who you are not based on the labels for your identity. Maybe use a personal experience to explain it, maybe just write a creative piece that incorporates the five senses (hear, see, touch, taste, and smell) to describe who you are. Then share your work and ask others if they new this about you.

Belen Mendoza

Belen Mendoza was born in Houston, TX in 1998. She had a decent childhood with a father that was loving, an amazing mother, and a caring sister and brother. Like every family, hers had problems but she sometimes saw things that a child shouldn't have seen. Her father would have his violent outbursts and beat her mother. Often times she would witness this and, at a young age, Belen felt alone. She looked forward to school just as an escape from the place she called home. Her mother had aspirations and dreams of her own. Even as a little girl it saddened her to see her mother give up those dreams. At times she noticed how her mother wanted to get away but stayed because she loved her daughters and son.

Apart from times like that she enjoyed her childhood: her father would brush her teeth as a child, take the family out, go on vacations etc. But everything must change. In April of 2009, her world took a 180 degree turn. As she was getting ready for another normal day in the fifth grade her mother received a call. A man she heard saying, "If he ever comes back I'll kill him." Could he be talking about her father? Brother? She learned it was her father. He had been having an affair and it had finally been revealed. Belen went to school and when she came back, like an act of magic, POOF! her father was gone. He moved out of the house and there went her happiness. Her now family of 3 battled with the depression and financial instability.

She went to middle school and was living a "nomadic" lifestyle, as she says. She moved from her home to her brother's apartment, back home, apartment, home, and then apartment again. The last time she lived in her home her parents finally decided to sell the house and break all ties. She couldn't be happier! During these six years it took her a lot of tears, courage, and strength and the faith she had in Jehovah to make her the strong woman she had become. She felt her childhood was cut short, but she's become a positive person and thankful that she learned from her experience. Thanks to the constant disappointments and no shows from her father, even not seeing him for months at a time without even a phone call, it's changed her.

You'd think that she became a rebel and spiraled out of control, but the complete opposite effect took place. She immersed herself into her studies and now is at the top of her class usually on honor roll. She does anything to make her mother proud. She's outgoing and always, always has a smile on her face. Even when she met Antonio, her best friend and loving companion, she gave him a semi-hard time. It took her about a year to let her guard down and trust anyone who wasn't her mother. As tough as she was, it should've pushed him away. Just like other guys who had come her way but he changed her life. But his persistence and caring attitude softened that guarded heart.

Now, Belen is trying to pursue her studies in Management Information Systems and is focusing on her academics with Genesys Works, a program that has opened so many doors for her that she didn't know existed. Belen has come a long way from where she started. She's hoping that through Barrio Writers she communicates to other youths that are going through similar situations that there is HOPE, there's more than the life that you are living right and if you don't like how life is right now, change it! Become the person you're aspiring to be and achieve your goals no matter if it takes sleepless nights, stressing, or even having Maruchan for dinner. It all becomes worth it at the end.

We Are One

We hug, and become one
just like we were sixteen years ago.
I feel your heartbeat
and my world suddenly starts moving slow.

I feel safe in your arms
even as a kid
you protected me from harm.
I see your struggles
I see your fears
Mama don't worry, I will always be there
wiping away your tears

I've become a parallel reflection of you
I am a warrior
I will win this battle for you
and the only reason is

Because I Love You.

Funeral

I caught your eyes at a funeral,
we were supposed to be feeling brutal
but you were being humorous
and then you called me beautiful,
I just knew you were being truthful.

Our connection was inevitable,
you stole my heart,
you were irrefutable.

I gave you a tough time
but strangely enough
you couldn't get enough.

<u>**Writing Activity**</u>
1. According to Belen, "Like every family, hers had problems…" What problems does your family have? What are the good things? How do the problems and good things make your family unique? List one of each and write a poem where you start with the problem and end on the good thing. How are they connected?

2. Each of us show love in different ways. Using Belen's poem 'We Are One' as inspiration, how does the person or thing you love give love to you?
3. Belen's poem 'Funeral' shows how we can find good things in dark places, such as romance at a funeral. Everything has at least two sides/stories to it. What's a dark place you're familiar with? Can you find any beauty in it? What's beautiful to you? Is there a dark side to it? Write a poem dedicated to these attributes.

Joanna Elizabeth Santos

My name is Joanna Elizabeth Santos and I was born on October 24, 1993. I was born in Los Angeles, California but grew up in a small town in Texas. I am unfortunately the middle child of three kids. Growing up in Texas away from my family was hard to adjust to and I never felt at place here. I'm currently a senior in college graduating with my Bachelor's degree in Communication Disorders on December 2015. I work two jobs to support myself and my planning addiction. My experience through college wasn't the greatest one but it taught me a lot. I hope to achieve great things in my life and make my parents proud.

This Isn't About You

You made my life hell all last year
I understood that you were angry
But did you have to do that?
Day after day. Night after night.
I cried and you probably rejoiced
Did you get some sick satisfaction?
Happy now?
Happy with your actions?
Are you okay that you emotionally ruined me?
You haunted me
Beautiful green eyes

Silky golden hair
Your smile when you saw me
Your arms were my home
My safe, happy place
I felt your arms grasp my body
And you just push me away
You really were the devil in disguise
Are you happy?
Are you fucking happy?
I fucked up, yes, but was it necessary?
I broke your heart and you broke mine
You felt betrayed, broken
How could she do that to me?
You thought
Was it necessary to degrade me?
Take advantage of the fact that you knew I wasn't okay
I've never let a man put his hands on me
Yet somehow I let you
I wish I could have gotten rid of you
I could have that night
Love blinded me
And it still does today
Despite the love I felt for you
I'm angry
Angry at you. Angry at myself.
You never should have done what you did
And I shouldn't have let you
It's over now
I got the strength to say
FUCK IT
And move on
I will never let that happen again
Not to me
You shaped me into the woman I am today
Strong
Independent
Life is happening without you
And here I am
Living and breathing
And guess what?

I'm just fine
See you controlled my future for so long
You were my future
I realized my future is without you
My future is great and it doesn't need you
It doesn't need anybody
I realized you weren't a need
You were a want
I control my future
I control my past
And I sure as hell control my present

I am

I am a set of two brown eyes
I am curly hair in the wind
I am tan skin in the summer
I am a daughter of two immigrants
I am Salvadorian American
I am a "guanaca"
I am a sister
I am a first generation college student
I am a woman
I am powerful
I am not a statistic
I am not a teenage mother
I am not a dropout
I am not a wetback
I am not submissive
I am strong
I am a leader
I am college educated
I am my own struggles
I am myself
I am not your stereotype

Writing Activity

1. Joanna chose to write to pieces of resistance, read each one and discuss what she is resisting against. How have you shown "resistance" in your life? **Resistance:** *noun*, the refusal to accept or comply with something; the attempt to prevent something by action or argument.

2. Is "resistance" negative or positive? Draw two columns, one labeled "negative" and the second column labeled "positive." List 10 examples of resistance in each column, then discuss how one example may be perceived as the opposite in which it is listed. For example, "taking time for yourself rather than with your family or partner," some may say it is selfish others may say it is self-care.

3. Check out the books *Poetry of Resistance* and *Cue the Writer: Cheers to the notion of Love, Hate, God, and Revolution*. If you can't get them, check out Marlon Lizama's poem "Immigrant's Poem" online: https://vimeo.com/56301223

    Then, write your own piece of resistance, talk about something you resist and have overcome, write boldly, unapologetically, tell us how it changed you or the way you see a certain situation.

Kevin Organista

Kevin Organista is a handsome young boy. He is 11 years old and his favorite music is rap and his favorite rapper is 50 Cent. He has a small sister and a mom. His mom has gone through many things and she is a very responsible mom. His favorite food is *sopes*. Kevin hopes to one day be an actor. Something Kevin would like to do with his extra time is play Basketball. Kevin's dream car is a Ferrari. One of Kevin's accomplishments was finishing Elementary. He also passed all of the missions in Call of Duty Ghost. Kevin is about to go to 6th grade. He will be attending Carr Intermediate, after that he hopes to go to Godinez High School, then he dreams to go to Stanford.

El Chamuco

My mom told me a story about my Abuelo/grandpa. It all started one night, it was around midnight and my great grandpa was playing and my great great Abuelos told him to go to sleep but he didn't want to. He started swearing so my great great Abuelo turned the lights off and left my great Abuelo alone. He sat down on the floor then he felt someone grab him in the ribs and he jumped, he was so scared. He turned on the light and there was nobody there so he screamed and ran into his parent's room. He was paranoid after that. He says that it was "el chamuco."

Nice Food

One day my tio took me and my mom to a nice restaurant. And it was filled mostly with white people. When some of them looked at me and my mom and my uncle they would make faces as if they had seen a pile of trash. That's why we left and just went to McDonalds.

Playing Doctor

When I was around four, me and my cousin also four, were bored so she told me if I wanted to play doctors. So I said yeah, and then she said that she was the doctor and I was the patient. I told her my stomach was hurting but we were just playing around. So she told me to grab a chair and to put it next to the refrigerator so I did that. She grabbed a little box of gummy bears and it was full. She told me to lay down on the bed but then she told me to never mind and stand up. Then she told me to eat all the gummy bears, so I chugged them down. Then I told her that I my stomach really hurt. I threw up a rainbow.

Police Brutality

I think we [society] should stand up for ourselves. The cops have been taking advantage of their jobs. Some cops kill people without a good reason and because they're racist. Now-a-days there is too much racism in law enforcement and cops. Cops should give us some space because they are everywhere. You can't even cross the street without seeing a cop. *MY NAME IS JEFF!*

<u>Writing Activity</u>
1. Do you have a story you want to tell that has been passed down from your grandparents, aunt, uncle or parents and why is it important for you to preserve the stories?

2. Find a poem, short story or even a music video that uses the cultural arts to express an emotion. Identify parts in the piece that connect to an emotion or "a form of being". Choose one emotion the piece uses and write a response to it. Simply write how you deal with that

emotion. Sometimes our reactions are uncontrollable, like tears, share your immediate reactions as well as your process reaction. What do you do to make yourself feel better or get through the feeling, and how do you reflect on it later?

Luis Flores

I am Luis Flores, a 17 year old raised in Guanajuato, Mexico and came to the US in 2004. Raised to a humble family, I strive to one day become a student in UNAM. My aspirations include dancing, drawing, graphic design, penmanship, engineering, coding and BMX.

To be drowned in euphoria. To be endowed with the knowledge of ones own potential. To be truly happy, and to admire ones own self and owns own image. This itself is an aspect of mans desires to be perpetually blissful and serene. This and more was what I held to myself. This is my description of my own happiness, and how for a moment I achieved a level of happiness and self-realization so empowering that it changed my life for the better; A chronological dysphemism that instilled peace within my future.

Young and ignorant. Privileged. Malevolent yet scared. These are the words that come to describe me prior to having my happiness and self identity discovered. A 7th grader, hedonistic and driven to live for the sole purpose of pleasure. Driven by a popular yet violent videogame title called San Andreas, the idea of a group, a gang, and to be given such trivial things by simply pursuing harming and negative goals. On the surface, my life was inspired by the violently frivolous nature and culture of the streets. My life seemed to be coming to an end. What purpose would I have? Why did the world need me?

In my left hand, I hold a weapon. A weapon, inspired and honed by a middle school ex-girlfriend who at the time illustrated an aesthetic so beautiful and iconic, my mere sketches could not compete or even compare, much less come close to pleasing her visual thirst for romantic arts.

My weapon in these streets was not tangible, yet it stood intangible. The byproduct of it was what could potentially change the world.
I wanted to pursue her. I did not want my middle school ex-girlfriend to leave me, for she became an idol. I strived to overcome her aesthetic skills and one day impress her. Even her name stayed etched inside my head. Carmen Sanchez.
Carmen was the safe haven from a life of blind aspirations and mediocre aspirations.
The light to my pitiful and…

Writing Activity

1. In his prose (which also serves as his bio), Luis explores his identity at one point in his life surrounding words that he would use to describe himself at the time, words that are both positive and negative. Think of yourself as you are now and write a list of words that describe you. Think of yourself a year ago, two years ago, or even five years ago, and make the same list. How do these list of words compare? How do you think that you have changed over time? Write a prose or spoken word piece that explores the present self, the past self, or both, perhaps illustrating how you have changed or grown as a person.

2. How can one's happiness over a relationship or a particular state of being spiral out of control? We see this in Luis's free form work, going from the bliss of his relationship and his art, to the violent idea of gang life and his hurt at being rejected. This creates a very surreal feeling, much like abstract visual art itself, where the forms don't exactly come together in the expected way, where paint drips from the page or where the colors or figures change from beautiful to grotesque. If you could think of a moment of your life, past or present, as a painting, what would it look like? How would you represent this on the page? Write a free form piece inspired by what you think your painting would look like.

Marcella Espinoza

Marcella Espinoza was born in Iowa yet raised in Santa Ana. She 15 years old and is a sophomore at Santiago High School. She lives with her parents and three sisters. Some of her favorite things to do in the free time is to read about previous cases dealing with police brutality. She is concerned about different things happening around the world. In the future she wants to help people with their problems. She wants to graduate high school and go to a four year university. She has accomplished many things and receives help from the Nicholas Academic Center. This is a program where tutors give you help when one needs it. She also attends every Friday to Coyolxauqui Circle, an open space to share her emotions.

Mi Familia

Laying on my bed
hearing the sound of my cousins playing outside
remembering my house being organized
The beds made
The kitchen clean
The house broomed and mopped
The chairs in their place
It was always like this
my mom always said

"nunca sabes cuando alguien venga a visitar"
When going outside it was a whole "new world"
Toys everywhere
Little kids running around
Just so loud outside
Watching my little cousins play
Gave me a sense of happiness
Happy to see our family together
Cause one my dad once told me
"No one can take family from you."

Writing Activity

1. Discuss among your group the misconceptions as a young person. What are the barriers and how do you tear them down?

2. Do you speak more than one language? If so, mix both or even three languages together through a poem or essay. Why is it important to have your language mixed in with other languages within your writing?

3. Narrate a family tradition and interview family members about a tradition or sacred family history and think of ways of exhibiting the end project to your family.

Jesús I'x Nazario

Jesús I'x Nazario was born on July 15, 2014. He is 20 years old. As a first generation Mexican-American he proudly owns both identities. Born in Houston, Texas, he has some appreciation of city life but prefers nature-esque locations. He loves green spaces. Maybe it's because he is the second oldest son of two warriors. Both of his parents are from the rural countryside in the state of Guerrero, Mexico. Currently, he is pursuing a double major in International Relations and Global Studies (IRG) and Journalism. He is going into his junior year at the University of Texas at Austin. He is part of two scholar's programs: the Senior Fellows and the McNair program at UT. He is also on track to pursue a PhD in Anthropology, a goal he plans on achieving in three or four years after finishing his undergraduate degree.

Jesús joined Barrio Writers in an attempt to learn from other youth and to improve his writing. He is satisfied with the results and hopes to continue experimenting with various writing styles outside of academia. He is aware that the future is a cloud of mystery but he knows one thing: he will continue traveling the world in order to further his learning, his ability to share stories, and to improve his love for writing as best as he can. After conquering Central America and Mexico, China is next in his world agenda, since he is learning Chinese Mandarin.

So far, all of Jesús' accomplishments have been possible with the help and support of friends, family, and inclusive environments like the Barrio Writers program. He is thankful for the opportunities that have come his way and will continue working diligently to also share opportunities and

become successful in all of his endeavors.
Adiós: a love letter

Uli,
I remember you like crazy.
With or without your *dientes de plata*
You always took a bite out of everything.
Your teeth tore a chunk of my heart, you know?
I bled for days. And after each day, I grew 10 years older.
I am now 300; I almost died.

I remember you *mijo*.
You were the middle child,
The joint of the family.
Your faint laugh was always the loudest.
We can't move now, you see?
Just soggy jigsaws waiting for the sun. For life.

You visited me yesterday, remember?
You grew taller, I had to stand on your stool.
The one you always used when you dived into your games.
Your bronzed texture was a pleasant sight.
Do you love the color brown, now?
Your long hair was down and raw like always.
It reminded me of Jesús, you remember him don't you?
I really liked talking to you yesterday, I hope you live in future dreams.

Remember when I tricked you to see the dentist?
Ha ha.
You were so innocent, so dumb!
With your small coffee-dyed eyes, you were too trusting.
You would've taken out the trash until your back curved,
But I never wanted to ask you that.
I didn't want to force you to stay.
sigh
I wish you had reached 18.

Do you forgive me, *hijo?*
Before you packed your 360°,
I forgot to say…you know.

"Please take care," was not enough.
Your signature tantrum made me mad.
You know I go blind when you're mad.

But I see you now, more vivid than in my dream.
You're smiling with your silver teeth,
Emitting light like the *luciérnagas* in our backyard.
My little warrior, you fight the darkness around you.

You will continue to defend,
And not just those crying.
I will see you again,
I miss you, my friend.

Until then,
Con amor y cariño,

Mamá

Writing Activity

1. In Barrio Writers, we don't ask our authors personal questions. Everything is fiction in our book. But we do ask, "What message would you like readers to get from your writing?" So, what message did Jesús give you with this piece? Is it really a love letter? What do you imagine the author meant when he wrote, "I wish you had reached 18." ?

2. Have you ever heard of the train called "The Beast," or "La Bestia" that runs through Mexico? Research it, here's a link to start your research: http://www.npr.org/sections/parallels/2014/06/05/318905712/riding-the-beast-across-mexico-to-the-u-s-border

3. After researching or watching one of the documentaries that covers stories about "La Bestia" and youth who ride it, write your own letter. It can be to a youth you read about or to the train itself, be creative, fill it with critical thinking, give the reader a message to offer solutions or get them to think differently of "The Beast."

Critical Thinking: a way of thinking — about any subject, content, or problem — in which the thinker improves the quality of his or her thinking by studying, judging, and reconstructing it. Critical thinking is self-directed, self-disciplined, self-monitored (in other words, it's up to you!), and self-corrective thinking. It includes effective communication and problem-solving abilities, as well as a commitment to overcome our personal opinions influenced by our family and/or society by studying both sides of an argument and adjusting your old ideas to include a new view of things.

Petra Jasmin Herrera

Born and raised in Houston, TX. I guess you could say I'm a Chicana because my parents are from Mexico. I don't think I've had any hardships throughout my life dealing with finance or housing or even family issues.

It's just that the one person I'm always fighting is me, myself, and I. And to be honest I hate not knowing who I am.

I write to figure myself out, to discover who's really inside this body of mine.

"Cliché Pain"

It's over used.
Perhaps overrated.

Love,
Hate,
Everything in between.

The feelings balled up inside us.
We shackled them up.
Tortured them.
Put them through pain of past memories.

And yet they still stand.
Wanting to explode.
To just outburst,
To scream and shout.

To be free.

Writing Activity
1. Labels can be hurtful and limiting, but they can sometimes also give us guidance and identity. For example, Petra, and many others, use the term Chicana (a woman born in the United States from parent(s) of Mexican or Mexican-American descent) to help them identify with a larger community. How do you identify yourself? What is your community? Write about how you see yourself in that community.

2. A cliché is an expression or idea which has become overused to the point of losing its original effect or meaning (for example: my love for you is like a rose, as wet as a fish, or as free as the wind.) However, Petra took a cliché (a poem about pain) and made it new, by showing how something cliché can be real. Take a cliché and make it new by showing us what it means to you either through a story or a poem.

3. What do you write for? Who do you write for? What confuses or angers you? Write about it. It can help you figure out who you are.

Hannah Hinojosa

Hannah Hinojosa is a Hispanic, 14-year-old freshman who attends Chaparral Star Academy. She is a competitive figure skater that was born and raised in Austin, Texas. Hannah is on a synchronized skating team in the Stars of Austin Figure Skating Club. She skates at the Chaparral Ice Rink and spends multiple hours there a week. Writing is how she manages her emotions when she is off the ice. In the future she wants to try out for the 2018 Winter Olympics

2018

I aspire to be
The likeable side of me
Scared but still strong
Rough but beautiful like a song
Hard work finally paying
Olympics now, no more playing

Doing what I love and that is skating
Best of the best now, that's my rating
Not sucking at life, I'm finally here

> Dancing on the ice, without a fear
> Using the applause as my fuel
> I hope future me will be this cool

Opening Your Voice

So basically, living with your parents is like trying to open a package of pencils after biting all your nails off. A fundamental component of the plan is missing and it isn't going to be easy. The opening of the pencils symbolizes the desire to open up your own voice. But when all your nails are bitten off like when parents disapprove of your voice, you'll find the opening of that package, more of a challenge. It's not like they mean to prevent you from finding your own voice. You guys just have different aspirations and different ideas of what living life looks like. And that's ok. It's normal for sons and daughter to have these disagreements but when they start pressuring you to be someone your not, your voice gets unobtainable in the process. This will make your quest to open that quest of pencils, more impossible. I know it might be frustrating. I know it might even hurt. But preservere in that challenge to open that box of pencils with your chewed off nails. It's all you got. It's all you need. Don't submit to what you don't believe in. Even if it's what your parents brainwashed you to. Open your own voice.

Changing the World

The world is a chaotic, neurotic place that insists on creating more and more ways to waste my time. New TV shows, new movies, more phones and less relationships. People would rather LOL to someone who's half way across the city, than pay attention to the person in their presence. There are more distractions in the world than there are things to be distracted from. If I had a chance to change the world I would fill that meaningless space with community and affection for people who aren't just an image on a screen.

How is a movie a date when the relationship with the strangers on the screen is where your chief concern is? What about the one who took time out of their day to spend time with no one else but you? Julia Roberts isn't going to give you that time. Jonny Depp isn't going to give you the love us humans desire in life. When the movie ends, so does your metaphorical relationship with the character on the biggie size screen. But look, the person next to you isn't going anywhere. What are you going to do about it? For 2 and a half hours you guys put each other on hold for what the world calls entertainment today. On this so-called 'date', no information about the other individual was obtained. Building relationships with others around you is never going to be easy. However, it's even harder to do when the world has made diving into distractions acceptable for time you attempt to spend with a real person. Real people are going to be there so much more than the faces on a screen on the apps on a phone.

If I could change the world, I would subtract mindless entertainment from the whole equations of getting to know others. Building community with others is where it is actually going to help us in life. I think the world will find talking to a friend when your alone, much more helpful than talking to your TV when your alone. Don't get distracted. Build those relationships.

Writing Activity

1. In her bio, Hannah states "writing is how she manages her emotions." How do you think writing has helped Hannah? Create a "How To Manage Your Emotions" column, under list ten ways to manage emotions, besides each suggestion write the emotion or emotions it might help manage. For example: "Running – Stress/Anger"

2. It is evident that Hannah used these three poems to "manage her emotions." Read them and discuss what emotions she is expressing in each piece. Then choose one piece to write a response. Write your own experience with the emotion you identified with, you can even write it in the same format as Hannah, or change it up completely! (Try hip hop, a different language, in the form of a Dr. Seuss poem, the format is up to you!)

Lily Risk

On the summer of July 7, 2002, Lily Risk opened her eyes and became apart of the world. As she grew up she discovered her love of sports and wanted to become an Olympic Athlete, and currently plays soccer and track. She currently lives with her Mom, Dad, Grandma, and three sisters, along with too many pets. She attends Holy Family Cathedral School and has many friends. She came to Barrio Writers to pursue her career of an author, and is looking forward to what is next in her life. Due to her crowded house she often tries to go out and hang out with her friends. One of her friends she often sees is Katelyn, and they enjoy making wacky videos together. Lily discovered a passion for art and at home she loves to draw, craft, or making cute decorations for her room. Lily loves her life at home, sports, and at Barrio Writers especially.

Eric Garner[1]

Words flash across a screen, announcing the unfair death of an innocent black man. Isn't it strange, a problem that started so long ago still isn't any better? The man whose life was taken away was Eric Garner, he was in New York and the police accused him of selling cigarettes without taxed

---

1   I wrote about this because I felt like this event really sparked a movement. This needs to be discussed more and can really help every one of different cultures unite.

stamps. Eric replied saying this was not true and he wished the police would stop harassing him. The police made a move and instinctively Eric swatted at the police. The Police grabbed him and put him in a chokehold, something they are not even allowed to do. Even after Garner repeated 11 times "I can't breathe", the police continued and in a matter of time, he was dead. After this event protest broke out everywhere, and people began to realize that the treatment was unfair and are taking action against police brutality. This man could have been a father, son, brother, or uncle. Due to these unnecessary actions, an innocent father and son, is now taken from his family. Police are supposed to be someone children can look up to, someone we can trust. Now our "role models" are killing innocent people. Already, we as a country, are taking a big step together to fix this problem. Maybe one day, all people despite their skin color can learn to respect each other, and we can all have equality.

Writing Activity

1. What is an ally? What are the traits of an ally? Are there things allies can and can't do?

2. Look up #BlackLivesMatter on Google and social media. How does a hashtag become a whole movement? Research the founders and their work that addresses justice for families like those of Eric Garner, Trayvon Martin and many others who have been killed by police.

    a) Alicia Garza
    b) Opal Tometi
    c) Patrisse Cullors

3. Like Lily, write a tribute to someone in the #BlackLivesMatter movement. Be creative, choose a leader or someone from the list above. Using the research you reviewed, write a counter-narrative to the media headlines.

    Counternarrative: a narrative that goes against another narrative. (i.e. "all teens are gang memebers and do drugs" – a story about a teen receiving a scholarship for college would be a counternarrative.)

Jasmine Capello

Jasmine Capello was born and raised in Austin, Texas. She lives with her little brother and sister along with Mami and Papi. Currently she attends Chaparral Star Academy entering sophomore year. She is one of Jehovah Witnesses, loves to draw and listen to music. In the future she plans to go to college in order to fulfill her goals.

How I Would Change The World

First of all, change is not always easy because not everyone will agree to the things that you do. If I can change something though it would be our Equal Rights, because not everything is fair. For example Mexicans strive for freedom here in the United States and a new life to change their mistakes in past times, but because of government laws and their issues in the U.S. people are not able to have this chance. I know that this is wrong. When I think of equality my mind automatically goes to the idea that people in general are limited to do the things they want because of their race, nationality, background, gender, or even your class. I can't wait for the day when the borderlines will disappear from the face of the earth and there is only one race, the race of mankind. Now I know this process of change will take more than one but that's how everything starts, with one, two, then three, and so on. We can all write a letter to the government and explain our opinions. This is a free country where we have freedom of speech so we should take advantage of that and express our feelings. Show them how we all can make a change together. Everyone.

Writing Activity
1. How would you define "equal rights"? Do you think everyone deserves equal rights regardless of gender, race, ethnicity or nationalism? Why or why not? Need something more specific? How about "gender inclusive restrooms on school campuses"?

    Note to Educators: We suggest using a marker or pen as a source of respect, whoever holds the object has the opportunity to speak freely without being interrupted. The object serves as a microphone. Also, tell the students the time set for this particular conversation 10 or 20 or 30 minutes? Once the set time is over, the conversation is over for the day. Setting parameters for respect and time keeps the conversation productive, speaking from experience. Also, once the conversation is over, it's a good time to follow up with a writing activity. Often, ideas keep flowing and can be caught on paper. ☺

2. If you could change one thing in the world, what would it be? If the world is too big to think about today, how about what you would change in your own community and why? What are the benefits to making such a change? Write in any form you like—poetry, hip-hop, Spanish, Vietnamese, Arabic, essay, short story, etcetera.

Diego Montaño

Diego Montaño was born in Santa Ana, California. He attends Valley High School and is part of the Nicholas Academic Center, Barrio Writers, and his school's ASB group. Diego aspires to graduate from high school to attend a University of his choice. He likes to draw and credits his older sister Marilynn for teaching him to draw when he was five years old. In his spare time, Diego takes an active role in his physical health and enjoys reading comics.

Soy Assesino

Mi nombre es Cruz de la Olla y soy asesino. Yo apenas cumplí 15 anos con una vida normal. Yo tenia mi mama, mi papa, mi hermano José, y mi hermana Camila. Un día mi papa se murió y nuestro mama comenso a tomar. Luego ella tenia un novio su nombre era Omar. Omar y nuestro mama comienzo a abusar y tortura a nosotros. Cada noche rezábamos a dios parque el los podía proteger los del diablo en la casa. Todos los días yo y mi hermano y mi hermana vivíamos con miedo el diablo estaba con nosotros. Día y noche, hora por hora los diablos estaba con nosotros. Un día luego cuando José y Camila regresaron del la escuela mi padrastro comienzo a pegar a mi hermano y mi hermana con su cinturón.

He began to hit them with his leather belt, whipping them, slapping them in the face, punching them in the stomach. Once I entered the house I saw how my brother and sister were bleeding from their face on the floor. Omar mi mero con sus ojos del diablo. Yo tenia mucho miedo pero mi hermano y mi hermana no estaban para ayudar and I had no choice but to kill him. I ran to the kitchen to get a knife and stabbed him in the leg before he could punch me in the face first. Omar estaba sagrando no podea caminar. He was on the floor struggling and I saw my little brother and my little sister struggling too. Jose garo una botela de cerveza y Camila garo un baseball bat. I had a knife filled with Omar's blood.

Luego, I whispered to him " tu vas a pagar binche diablo". Mi hermano began to hit him with the beer bottle and my sister smashed him down with the bat as I continued to also hit him. All of our weapons were filled with blood. La sangre de el diablo, el estaba muerto. Despues mi mama entro en la casa and the whole living room was filled with wreaking with the sangre del diablo. Cuando ella entro nuestra mama nos iba a matar también pero mi hermano stabbed her in the back. The cops came and we were all arrested for murder.. Y yo declare a los policías que yo era el assesino. I went to juvy leaving my brother and sister in daycare. Cuando yo cumplí 18 anos fue a recoger a mis hermanos y nos fuimosmuy lejos. Donde nadie superia la verdad que mis hermanos tambien fueron los asesinos. Soy Cruz de la Olla. Soy el assesino.

Writing Activity
1. Do you read any science-fiction or any legends? Is there a favorite story you'd like to write about with a twist of adding the themes of culture and identity.

   Science-Fiction: a genre of speculative fiction that deals with imaginative concepts which includes time travel, advanced technology, space travel, and extraterrestrial life.

   Legend: a traditional story sometimes popularly known as historic but unauthenticated.

2. Are there any television shows or movies that inspire you to write a suspenseful story? Write a twist to the end of the plot or maybe add characters based out of friends and family in your life.

3. In your group, create a legend or a fictional character that has all the qualities your group has write a collective story. Or create a superhero based out of the multiple people that inspire you in your life and how would they live?

Carlos Amaya

Carlos Amaya was born on May 5, 1998 in Houston, Texas and currently lives there. As of now, he is 17 years old and is a junior in high school. He lives with his family and only has one sibling, a younger brother. He was introduced into the Barrio Writers program as a result of being in the Academic Achievers program, which aims to get minorities into college.

Both of his parents came from Latin American countries, with his father coming from El Salvador and mother from Mexico. They came to America at very young ages after their parents brought them in the search for greater economic and social opportunities.

My Future

As a teenager, I often see myself as someone who wants to change the world in a positive manner, however large or small that change may be. Positive change has been found and created in multiple ways by different people, but I personally want to influence change through technological innovation.

For as long as I can remember, I have been intrigued and amazed by all types of computerized devices, and have always sought to learn about how such objects work and how their parts fit together into a cohesive whole, able to improve and impact the quality of someone's life. Oddly enough, throughout my childhood I didn't know what I wanted to do when I got older. It wasn't until my aunt introduced me to various careers during my freshman year that I began to realize the answer had been there throughout my entire life. The moment I discovered and learned about computer engineering, I knew it was the right career for me. Not only would I be able to be around technology, but I would be able to design it as well.

My goals for the future include becoming a computer engineer and perhaps starting a business in the future. I ultimately want to give back to not only my community, but the rest of the world as well.

Writing Activity

1. Carlos has a goal on how to give back to his community. What are your future goals? How will you give back to your community? If you don't know yet, that's ok! Discuss with family and/or friends about your future goals and see if you can all give back to your community.

2. Where are your parents from? How did they meet? If you don't know or can't ask, that's ok too! Write a short story about how you think your parents met. It's fine if it's not true. What's important is that you gain a deeper understanding of your roots.

3. How does technology affect your life? Write a story about a future where everyone has access to this technology. OR write a story where only a few people have access to this technology and no one else does. Google the terms Utopia and Dystopia.

Armani Scott

Name is Armani. I'm currently 16 years of age. Born in Atlanta but raised in Nacogdoches, Texas so I consider myself an eccentric southern belle. I dance, write poetry, do yoga, read, and cook for fun. Poetry is my passion though because it's where I feel most free. To me, the most important thing I think my audience should know is that I'm a young African American feminist. Just being that, I have a million stereotypes against me but I continue to rise from the ashes in rebirth.

"I'm going to live life unapologetically, because I'm proud of who I am, and I'm not going to apologize for who I am anymore." —Ingrid Nilsen

Forbidden

Let me break what we have down in the most loving way possible. Give me the chance to touch your mind poetically before I touch you physically. Can I have your mind for a brief moment?
See, me, I am the earth. Call me "Mother Nature." I am the African queen that resides in the Promise Land from that book. Their "Bible." You can find me in the heart of any jungle where peace and serenity is harbored. You can find traces of me in hidden spots on beautiful islands. I am in fields of wild flowers and in the most sacred parts of the desert...
But you? You were a galaxy to me. Much bigger than my small little planet. Everything about you held me together. It holds me up. Your stars,

your meteor showers, your many glorious moons, and inhabitable planets, in orbit with me. All of that holds my pieces together. That great force that you have—gravity—that keeps me sane. Because, see, without it I would go spinning away into the darkness, and swept away, and in pain.

The only thing is, unlike me, you're not accepted. No trace of you in their world, we're forbidden. Like the fruit in the garden of the man and woman that were created with sin from their magic man in the sky…our forbidden love is hidden. Not to be shouted out loud from the highest mountaintops. Just whispered in the rare moments that I find your arms wrapped around me and your words around my cold, but warming, heart…your galaxy is not supposed to have a connection to my nature, according to the them and their books, but love is stronger than any person or any one thing, so let me break down what we have in the most loving way possible. Give me the chance to touch your mind poetically before I touch you physically. *Can I have your mind for a brief moment?*

Struggle

There's beauty in our struggle
We struggle for love
And for success
For the fame and the fortune
And all the rest
We struggle and we stress
Trying to do our best
Trying to get a confirming "yes!"
Yes, you did it. Yes, you won.
Without getting locked up
Without having a daughter
Or a son…
And even then in this life of sin,
Someone points a gun
Points a gun in intimidation
In fear and in ignorance
But ignorance is bliss,
Especially if you just get a slap on the wrist
But there's still beauty in our struggle
Even if that policeman is a bitch

Animal

You capture me.
I am vulnerable.
You claw at my heart.
I wince in pain,
But I welcome you.
You cause me so much pain,
But I look over that.
You ask, "Do you love me?"
I answer honestly.
You say, "Then we'll be fine."
"I'll make it up to you."
I swear I heard this every time.
Every time you cheated.
Every time you disrespected me.
Every time you acted like you didn't care.
I loved you through it all.
Time after time.
I took you back,
But you kept your piercing grip on me.
You kept your vicious claws in my heart.
Nails digging deeper,
Blood spurting,
My heart is hurting!
STOP!
Don't hurt me again…
I beg you.
I plead with you.
I can't take it anymore
Don't hurt me.
I can't be your victim anymore.
Yourpreyonmyfearandmyquickbeating
Heartasitrytotellyoutoloosenyourclaws
Onmyheartmywordsruntogetherandistutter
and-andistopandmywordsoverlapasitellyouto
STOP!
I'm vulnerable…
Your claws in my heart…
I stop breathing.

I succumb to your darkness.
I lose myself…
You feel victory…
My heart becomes numb…
In my pain I die…
In death I lose feeling…
And in losing feeling from you…
I am free.

You're Trying

(you're trying)
to be perfect
(you're trying)
to be good
(you're trying)
to be what they want
(you're trying)
to be beautiful
(you're trying)
to fit society's standards
(you're trying)
to be "happy"
(you're trying, you're trying)
(you're dying…)
but they don't even know

To My Dancing Mom, From Her Dancing Daughter

When I was weeeee high
You put me in your old boots and hat

I've been a Dragonette at heart all along
Because of you

In elementary school, we took trips to football games
There is where you instilled my love for halftime shows

I've been a Dragonette at heart all along
Because of you
During middle school, when I tried out for pom squad
You showed me all your tricks
To getting high kicks

I've been a Dragonette at heart all along
Because of you

Now I'm in high school,
A Dragonette through and through
Thank you for encouraging me
To be the best dance I could be

Writing Activity

1. Read all of Armani's poems, which one is your favorite? Why? How do you connect with it? Which one do you connect with the least? Why?

2. Check out Nikki Giovanni's poem "Ego Tripping," then compare it to Armani's piece "Forbidden." Visit this website: http://feministing.com/2013/12/17/watch-nikki-giovanni-perform-ego-tripping-on-melissa-harris-perry/

   In what ways is Armani's work similar to Nikki Giovanni's? In what ways is it better?

3. In creative writing, copying is not plagiarism, it is creative work (In an essay it's plagiarism, just a reminder.) Take a few lines from each poem and write your own "ego tripping" piece, then go back and change the lines you copied and make them your own. Share them with your peers, share them with Barrio Writers at we will post it on our blog!

Jake Malvaiz

My name is Jake Malvaiz. I'm 16 years old. I was born on July 21, 1998 in Austin, Texas. I'm the second kid of my family, I live with my six brothers, my mom, my aunt, and my three cousins. My real name is Eric Malvaiz but I like to call myself Jake because people laugh and bully me because I can't say my name well because I'm hearing impaired. I like to dance a lot and I also going to be leader of my dance group but I might have trouble working alone. So I'm gonna need an adult to work with me. I'll also join a big group called Young Life (YL) during four years of college, I'm going to be YL leader and study to be a film director.

Jake & Izzy

Jake: Hey Izzy, did you remember when we met.
Izzy: Yeah I remember.
Jake: I feel so shy to met you and I never have a guy help me out to pick my stuff before.
Izzy: Well it was good to help you out because we are all here to make new friends.
Jake: Did you remember when I asked you where you been all day and I haven't seen you everywhere.
Izzy: Yeah I remember and I told you that I'm really busy and sometime I'm at the back of the Mill.
Jake: Oh I didn't know you go to that building…What about free time

	wanna hang with me?
Izzy:	We aren't allowed to go during free time.
Jake:	Did you remember the day when we throw the party?
Izzy:	Yeah I remember.
Jake:	Did you remember when you told me to try the dry pickle?
Izzy:	Yeah I remember when I told you to try it.
Jake:	Yeah, about that, I don't like them.
Izzy:	What? You should try them.
Jake:	I don't like pickle.
Izzy:	Hey Jake!! Would you like me to show you what I do?
Jake:	Yeah that be fine to me.
Izzy:	Did you like me to show you now or later?
Jake:	It doesn't matter to me.
Izzy:	Ok let go.
Jake:	Did you remember when you show me where your work?
Izzy:	Yeah I remember.
Jake:	It was awesome when you show me inside and it was awesome that I didn't know you wash the dishes for us.
Izzy:	Yeah I wash every single plate y'all eat.
Jake:	Well thanks for washing the dishes for us.
Jake:	Did you remember when I ask you to come to my cabin?
Izzy:	Yeah I remember and I did.
Jake:	I'm so glad you came but I feel embarrassed when you watch me cry with my leader Henry.
Izzy:	I remember when I walked to you and said "Hey Jake."
Jake:	I remember when I said "Hey Izzy" I turn my face down fast because I feel so embarrassed to see me cry.
Izzy:	I remember when your leader told you "Did you want to walk with Izzy" and you said "Yes"
Jake:	I remember when you told me your story and it was beautiful. I'm glad you shared with me.
Izzy:	Yeah I remember and I'm glad you like it.
Jake:	Did you remember when you took me back to my cabin?
Izzy;	Yeah I remember. Did you remember the golf cart?
Jake:	Yeah It was totally cool that I never seen someone took me back to the cabin with the golf cart. Thank for take me back to my cabin and thank for help me feel more better.
Izzy:	Yeah no problem. See you tomorrow!
Jake:	Ok see you tomorrow
Jake:	Did you remember when we took pics of us and my friends?

Izzy: Yeah I remember.
Jake: Hey Izzy, you know every time I see you, you always surprise me and I'm really happy that you always there for me.
Izzy: I love to meet you and yeah man I'm happy to be your friend.
Jake: You make me cry...I never ever have a friend like this before and I like to share with you my favorite bible verse Psalm18:2.

Writing Activity
1. Have you ever been friends with someone who is hearing impaired? What about with other types of physical challenges? Why or why not?

    A hearing impairment is a hearing loss that prevents a person from totally receiving sounds through the ear. If the loss is mild, the person has difficulty hearing faint or distant speech. A person with this degree of hearing impairment may use a hearing aid to amplify sounds.

2. Do you think Jake (Eric) should have to change his name to make those who can't understand him feel more comfortable or accepting of him? What can we do as a society to make him feel more comfortable with his name or being himself? As a group, create public announcements that educate youth and adults about several physical challenges that you see in your community. Promote acceptance and give them options on how to befriend a person with such challenges.

3. Is there a special friendship in your life that has helped you get through a touch time? Like Jake, write down a conversation, which helped you overcome a bad day or get through a touch time. Sometimes we just need to read other's experience to realize we are all human and sometimes we all need an unconditional friend to remind us.

Mireya Del Rocio Ortiz

My name is Mireya Del Rocio Ortiz. I'm 16 years old and was born and raised in Houston, TX. I live with both of my parents, Rocio y Ernesto Ortiz. My father works extremely hard to always provide a roof over our heads and food on our table, leaving my mother behind to take care of my five siblings including myself. Sad to say that most of our family time is spent with my mother, although I understand my father's circumstances. I am pursuing a career as a Petroleum Engineer, so that my Latino community won't be another statistic.

Mi Todo

Mi Jefa, la que me saca las canas.
My Mama, quien me da las ganas.
Mi Cuyilla, la más querida.
Mi Ama, la que me hace las quesadillas.
Mi Vida Entera, lo digo por las tortillas que se echa.
Mi Adoracion, por toda la motivación que me entrega.
No miento cuando digo gracias por ser mi razón de ser.

Writing Activity
1. What does it mean to be 'another statistic?' What does that mean to you? How will you not be 'another statistic?' Write a poem of what being a statistic means and how you will not become one.
2. Who or what is your todo (your everything)? What nicknames do you have for them/it? Why? Write a poem outlining those nicknames and what they mean to you.

3. Who in your life works really hard? Do you know why? Take a day in their shoes and write what they work for at the end of that day.

Leslie Lawyer

Leslie Lawyer was born on September 21, 2002 and raised in Santa Ana, California. She is in the 7th grade and likes to write about her past and future. In the future she would like to be an actor on film. Some of her favorite hobbies include acting, singing, hair styling and trying different things. Leslie wants to go to a college that focuses on acting and film. Her struggles are she needs to wait 5 more years and have to take practice acting classes to start early. My family is Mexican however from my Dad's side they are Black Hispanics, born in the U.S. My mom was born in Mexico but all together we are a mix of White and Black Mexicans but I feel Mexican. I live with my mom's family of 10 people along with my dog named Jasmin.

You

You're selfish, I'm helpful
You're having fun, while I'm helping
You're busy eating, while I'm busy sharing
I am friendly, you are greedy
I'm clean, you're dirty
I'm sweet, you're mean
You like music, I like music
I like boys, you like boys
I'm picky, you're picky

I'm neat, you're neat
I'm cheesy, you're cheesy
I like movies, you like movies
We are best friends

Respect

I think it's stupid to give respect to white people when they do something bad unless you give the same respect to black people when they do something bad. It's disrespectful when white people have more money because their parents in the past got everything they wanted. When black people had to fight for everything they wanted and now they still have to fight for what they want. Fight for their lives, justice and respect.

Writing Activity

1. What does respect mean for you? Have you felt disrespected for your culture, skin or language? Write in ways that moment made you feel and write the pride you have in your culture, skin, or language.

2. Research on topic below, find 3 pieces of information that you have not studied in school on that topic.

    a. Bracero Program
    b. Selma to Montgomery March
    c. Japanese Internment

Catheryne Molina

Her imagination ran free. Unable to tame it, she let it be.

Catheryne Molina was born on July 26, 1999 in Houston TX. She was the youngest out of five daughters. She is also a first generation American; she was the first to be born in the United States. So that means she was supposed to be the first to go to college and experience all these new things, without really having someone to guide her through it.

She enjoyed writing, reading, drawing, painting, and in general, just creating. She liked to let her creative side out and just created all of these crazy stories and drawings. She liked going with the flow and let what happened, happen. If something bad would happen, then she would just suck it up and deal with it.

She grew up with her mother telling her to be strong and not let people take advantage of you. She always thought that her mother was exaggerating. She didn't think of people being that evil and manipulative, but then she learned. She learned that not all people are good. She learned that some people just use other people to get what they want. After that she grew stronger. She grew stronger for herself and for others. She saw that other people were going through some of the same stuff she went through, so she decided to take her writing and drawing skills and put them to use. She started writing a message that said "You are who you are, you are strong even if you think you're weak, you have many talents even if you think you're worthless, never let anyone make you less." She became stronger and started fighting for those who thought they weren't strong.

True Colors

The world was black and white. There were rules and regulations that everyone had to stand by. Everyone was told to act and dress a certain way. If you were different then you would be shunned.

There was a girl. She seemed like everyone else. She followed the rules and regulations. She acted like a proper young lady, but that was just a mask she wore. Underneath, she was a completely different person. Underneath her black and white appearance laid color.

She had light brown hair, green, sparkly eyes, rosy pink checks, and lightly tanned skin. She knew for a long time that she wasn't like everyone else, but she feared. She feared of being shunned and persecuted by other people. She had to disguise her true self with black and white makeup so she could fit in.

One day while walking her normal route to school, she bumped into someone. After they bumped into each other she took a few steps back, trying to compose herself. When she looked up to see who she had bumped into, he was gone.

As she was about to start walking again, something caught her eye. There was a single flower on the ground, but this flower wasn't like the rest. This flower had color! It looked like a light pink rose.

As she looked at the light pink rose and thought about the person who dropped it. It looked so precious and rare. She would have never thought that flowers could have any color. She knew that anybody would be upset to lose something like that.

She looked at where the boy was heading when they bumped into each other, then started walking towards that direction. She didn't really see the boy when they bumped into each other, but she did know that he had a black hoodie with a big, white letter "A" on the back.

She started scanning the street, trying to find the boy with the white letter "A" hoodie on. She looked through many street and roads trying to find him. As she was about to give up on trying to find the boy, she spotted a big white letter "A" on a black hoodie walking a couple of blocks away.

She started running towards where she saw the letter. Soon enough she caught up with the boy in the hoodie and tapped on his shoulder. He turned around, and as he did she was shocked of what she saw.

The boy had color! He had bright blue eyes, dark brown hair and light brownish skin. "Is there something you need?" he asked while looking at the girl.

She never knew that there were other people that had color like she did. She always thought people were black and white, and that she was a wolf in sheep's clothing.

She tugged on his hoodie, making him follow her to a back alley. She stopped in front of the boy. She then lifted the pink rose and asked "Did you drop this?" He looked shocked and started to feel around his big hoodie pocket.

He then looked at the girl and asked, "Yes. Where did you find it?" She handed him the flower and answered, "Well we bumped into each other and I saw it on the ground. It just looked so beautiful and rare that I thought that if I was the one who lost this" she points at the rose. "I would be very upset, so I've been looking around trying to find you."

He looked at the flower and then back at her. "So, you went through all that trouble to give this back?" she just nodded. "Well..." he started to speak, "Since you went through all that trouble. I would like you to have this." He hands her the pink rose and she looks at him with a confused expression. "Really!?" she asked. He just nodded and said, "Yes, and you know, you should really take off that makeup."

He then rubs the sleeve of his hoodie against her face. Exposing her real colors. She just stood there in shock and asked, "How did you know I was wearing makeup?"

He smiled and said, "Because I was once like you." She gave him a confused expression and asked, "What do you mean?"

"I used to hide myself from people and wore a disguise in order to fit in. Then I realized I was going nowhere if I kept living a fake life."
She looked at him and asked "But weren't you scared of what people were going to say and that they were going to shun you for being different?"
He smiled at the girl and answered, "Yes, to be honest. I was scared, but then I learned that being different isn't such a bad thing. Yes, there will be those people who won't like it and leave your life, but those people don't matter. The ones that do matter are the ones that accept who you really are and will stay by your side no matter what."

The girl the pulled down her sleeve and rubbed of the rest of the makeup off. She then smiled at the boy and said, "You're right. I'm going to stop being someone I'm not and show my true color!"

... and with that she went out to the world showing her true self, showing her true colors.

Writing Activity

1. What's a lesson, saying, or dicho that you have heard? Where did you hear it or from whom? Do you live by it? Why or why not?

2. Catheryne's story is full of descriptive passages for her characters, such as, "She had light brown hair, green, sparkly eyes, rosy pink cheeks, and lightly tanned skin," and "he had a black hoodie with a big, white letter "A" on the back." Describe a person in your life or a character you've created like this, using at least two pieces of their clothing and two features of their body. What does it say about them? Their world?

3. Catheryne's story is very similar to a fable or, a story conveying a moral. Use that lesson/saying/dicho and character description and combine them. How does that character live in a world that lives by that lesson/saying/dicho?

Diana Hernandez

Diana Hernandez was born in Houston, Texas on December 4, 1999 and is 15 years old. Her parents were born and raised in Mexico. She is the youngest of three girls and enjoys playing the guitar during her spare time. Diana was recently awarded for her outstanding work in her English class. She is currently in the Harris County Sheriffs Office (HCSO) Explorer Program and hopes to pursue a career in law enforcement.

Education

I wake up to my mom shaking my arm saying "mija levántate ya vas tarde dile a tu hermana que te lleve a la escuela antes de irse al trabajo." At this point, I already know I missed the bus.

As I rush to get ready I hear her say, "bye, ya me voy, que te valla bien en la escuela." On my way to school, my sister lectures me saying "no es la culpa de mom que te levantes tarde" and that I should go to bed earlier.

All I thought about at that moment is about how worried my mom must have been because I might miss class time. She always says "la escuela va primero" and that's because she grew up in a little town in Mexico where schools were limited, so she was only able to get a third grade education. My mom repeated third grade two times because she loved school and was excited to learn new things. Eventually she stopped going because there was too many kids and not enough room for more students. She never owned a real backpack, only a plastic bag, one pencil, and a notebook. She took care of her school supplies because she knew that if she lost them she would not be able to get more any time soon.

As I walk through the school doors I realize how lucky I am to be in ninth grade, which is far beyond the education she received.

Writing Activity

1. What accomplishments are you proud of? Keep in mind that accomplishments don't have to be recognized by your school or parents or anyone except you. Why are you proud of it? Write a story about what that accomplishment was, the work it took to achieve it, and why it means so much to you.

2. When Diana had to start waking herself up early, she realized she had to 'grow up' and take responsibility for her actions. What moment did you realize you had to 'grow up?' Write a story of that moment. How does that moment affect you today?

3. As Diana learned with education, we all have things we are lucky to have. What are you lucky to have? Why are you lucky to have it? Who doesn't have it? Write a paragraph describing it and what you plan to do with that opportunity.

Ariana Espinoza

Ariana Espinoza was born on February 2, 2003 in Sioux City, Iowa. She was only in Iowa for three months and then moved to California where she was raised for most of her childhood. She is now a young 12 year old and lives with her fantastic parents and three sisters. She's a 7th grader at Doig Intermediate in Santa Ana, Ca. Some of her interests include reading, art, and writing. Her dream goals are to go to Santiago High School and be able to graduate in order to go to a University. She aspires to become a future doctor.

Mi Linda Casa

When you open the door to my house
you could see the bright white walls all clean
glistening from top to bottom
You could see the picture frames fade black to brown
Entering the kitchen you could smell fried peppers and chicken
silver pots sitting on the stove with low heat as its simmering gently
In distance you could see the sunset
shimmer in red, yellow, and orange
Out in the balcony where the fresh air touches your face
You could hear my loud sister screaming saying "ma!", "pa!" every time
Every face inside is always happy with a smile that shines as bright as a star

A Special Someone

Family is not just from same blood
It's about people that care about you
receive you for who you are
Someone smart
Someone loyal
Someone kind
Someone helpful
Someone that actually cares about you and doesn't judge you for who you are
Family is like a key to life
Family is something that no one can ever take away from you
Not in a year or even in a million years

Writing Activity

1. Define home in a poem or essay form. Expand beyond the literal term because home can be more than just a physical location. Home can be a person, place or thing. Does it travel with you? Is it something you eat or a tradition passed down to you by your family or friends?

2. What does community mean to you? Is there a group or person that supports you? Consider your classroom a community and how do you all support one another? Discuss with your group member and create a collective poem that brings all of your voices together.

> **Identity:** i·den·ti·ty, *noun*, the fact of being who or what a person or thing is.
>
> **Culture:** cul·ture, *noun*, the arts and other manifestations of human intellectual achievement regarded collectively (i.e. food, music, language, clothing)

Tobin Gonzales Mahlke

I am Tobin Gonzales Mahlke but everyone calls me Tobin. I was born on June 17, 2002. I have three dogs and two fish. I have a friend named Eli who plans on becoming a soccer player in England and I'll be his manager. I dedicate this story to Capcom and all of you gamers, nerds and geeks. I'm a geek and proud!!

Who Am I?

Black, all I see is black…never ending blackness. It's been this way forever. I can't feel or see anything, but this time it's different somehow. All I can remember is thinking, "who am I?" and then I wake up from what seems to have been a dream. I can't remember anything, everything's numb. I stumble and fall as something starts to run towards me.

As I look, I feel calm when she picks me up. I ask, "Who are you"? She says she's my mom and that we're going outside to go fishing. We walk outside and the sun is beating on the wet grass, as it glimmers, causing me to look away. My eyes burn as we walk into the woods. I ask more questions, trying to find out who I am…but start to get fewer answers. I ask if she can put me down, I try adjusting to the weight of myself while we keep walking. Finally we make it to the spot and I see a young girl, a middle aged man and a baby as I sit on a rusty old rocking chair…squeak, squeak, squeak.

I stare into the murky green swamp like pond…waiting. I ask mom who the man is and she says it is a friend of hers. I look at him and see that he looks dirty but seems strong. His clothes are ripped, stretched out and faded from the sun. I realize he is a farmer and a father. I look at my mom and ask, "Do I have a dad"? I notice she's crying as she opens her mouth, but then there's a tug and a bite so I go for my fishing line. The fish takes it and then bites mom's and takes her bait too. I see a disturbance in the water as a thin fin splits through the green murk, heading away…I look at mom, she looks at me, and we start giggling, as we get ready to head home.

Writing Activity

1. What stood out to you about this story? Is there a particular moment you can connect to, maybe a fishing trip of your own or an absent parent you have wondered about? Why do you think this story seems longer than what it really is?

2. Using the brevity (shortness) of this story as a goal, write your own childhood memory or first fishing trip. Describe the little details greatly and lightly add a bigger story that connects to personal emotions. Remember, everything is fiction in Barrio Writers, so it doesn't necessarily have to be true or it can be, and we will never know if it is. ☺

3. Once you have your "throw up on paper"—as we like to say in Barrio Writers instead of a "very rough draft"—go back to it a few days later and make your story longer, making the emotions seem like the real story, it's not just a memory or a fishing trip, it's a moment in life that changed the main character's perspective.

Odalis Espinoza

Odalis Espinoza, a 17-year-old young lady born March 12, 1998 in Sioux City, Iowa. God was able to gift her with a wonderful family. Her parents are very supportive that they have guided her in the path to success. She hopes that her three younger sisters are able to see her as a role model.She is currently a Senior at Santiago High School in Garden Grove, California. Through her hard work she has been able to maintain her grades and balance her life as well. Despite having come from a low income family she has been able to receive resources in her community that have allowed her to show her potential. The Nicholas Academic Center (tutoring center) located in Santa Ana has allowed her to be able to expand her knowledge. She has had the opportunity to go to Washington D.C. for a Law Camp and attend a pre-college program at the University of Notre Dame thanks to the NAC who have believed in her. One day she hopes that she will be able to give back to her community. She would like to be able to see change in her community for the better. Many people were able to invest in her future so she would like to do the same.

Soy

Soy mujer, soy chicana,
Pero sobre todo soy libre,
Libre para ser alguien diferente
Libre para romper las reglas de la tradición

Libre para tomar mis propias decisiones
Libre para expresarme
Libre para luchar por mis sueños
Libre para soñar sueños sin importancia
Libre para volar hacia lo imposible
Libre para escribir mi historia
Libre para vivir mi vida
Pero sobre todo libre para tener una voz.

English:

I am a woman, I am a Chicana
But more importantly I am free
Free to be someone different
Free to break away from the traditions
Free to make my own decisions
Free to express myself
Free to fight for my dreams
Free to be able to dream nonsense
Free to fly into the impossible
Free to write my own story
Free to live my life
But more importantly I have the freedom to have a voice.

Writing Activity

1. Here's a Barrio Writers free writing prompt: What does culture mean to you? Don't worry about grammar or spelling.

2. Odalis wrote "Soy" which translates to "I am". Write your own version of "Soy".

3. Research revolutionary women of color with your group. How have they shaped history and do they inspire you to create change within your community?

    a) Comandanta Romana
    b) Harriet Tubman
    c) Modesta Avila

Diego Flores

Diego Flores was born on June 17th in Houston, Texas to devout (relatively) liberal Roman Catholic Mexican-American parents Maria Cruz Flores and Rafael Narciso Flores. He now lives with both of his parents, Lobo (a dog), Rafael Flores (a brother), Sarah Flores (a sister), Mellie Nataha Cruz (a cousin –like-a-sister), and Maria Hernandez (a grandmother [mother's mother]). Growing up, Diego hated reading but that soon changed when Rebecca Morales (a cousin-in-law who's more like cousin and less in-law) introduced him to *A Wrinkle in Time* and Diego's mother forced him to read the whole book. Yet he still hated writing until at age 12, Diego realized that he's queer. In order to filter out the confusion, he began to keep a journal. But having a daily journal entry proved to be difficult. So instead he wrote poetry as a way to encode his writing. Since then he has used words as a haven as mental illness also began to seep into his life leading him to be admitted into a psychiatric hospital on April 19, 2015 where he stayed for ten days. Now his life isn't perfect (he's taking credit recovery classes for Algebra for example) but he's moving forward, dreaming of one day changing the world with his writing and to write even better in Spanish than Pantaleon Flores (his grandfather (father's father), who's also a poet.

Angels

Holy we are told we are
Children of God!

Favored above all creations
Every religion, group, and people seem to say
Great and mighty is the human!
The only species with a soul!
Grand and tall our people stand
But others… they seem to slouch
They have their eyes cast down, quit below all the ruckus
For they know, **they know**
Of the sins Homo Sapiens have done
Tainted the history of our earth since our birth eons ago
They realize that we are not angels, but they make a grave mistake
When they categorize us as demons
We are not all vile, corrupt immoral creators
But neither are we purely virtuous, divine beings
We are the Purgatory
We wish for a little of Heaven and Hell
We are the Fey
Borne of angels and demons
Tricky littlie faeries we are
Using our magic to do our bidding
We put up a veil that hides the demon underneath
Or perhaps a saintly angel
Or something in between.

O human
Who are thee?
Are you like an angel?
A noble, holy being
Or are thee a demon?
A malicious, malevolent thing
Neither is the answer
We, really, just a mix of both
With something new, never before seen
We are the Fey
Having the potential for both
And if we combine our forces we transform and transform our earth
To rise to the Heavens
Or be buried alive in Hell.

So what we must do is push the demon(s) within us

Out and down so that they may descend to Hell and crumble to dust
And let the angel(s) within us bring us to our thrones in Heaven above.

Beautiful Ashes

I sit on the pinewood fence entranced with the moon
Her waxy face melting, the drops stinging and soothing upon my tempestuous face
I can feel it trying to crawl into my ears
Trying to block out the honey from lullabies of the she-beasts
Starburst scales in the noxious bayou
Surrounded by the sharp blades of the dancing green grass below
But I stab my eardrum with my pointer fingers with such a force that I crash
Hands cut down
Back anything but straight
Neck bruised
Knees too stiff to kneel
I crawl toward them as they beckon me over with their wings
Dark and shiny
As if a rainbow was hiding under their rough skin
Their lips so plump and pink and irresistible
I can imagine the chill down up my spine as their claws glide along my bare chest
Until the boy covered in pollen kisses me
His silver eyes brighter than any sun
His lips sweeter than any honey
And when his tongue enters my mouth I want to scream from the surge of clarity
How my heart pumps hypocrisy into my veins
But the sirens roar
I know the only way to stop the pumping of chaos is to rip my heart out
But I can't now as he pushes me up the fence
Growling and clawing at my body
Thirsty for my moan
And o, do I give it to him
The vodka, pills, hate and clarity aside for now
Tonight I'm his.

On the patio

Bite your mangoes, don't drink or burn them
Smell the cherry blossoms dance
On the patio of the sky's psychotic romance
Feel the array of colors pull you right on the mud
Red twirling her dress till it's as green as your blood
Taste my words rip through sky and earth
Making Heaven and Hell crash into each other like a 'heterosexual' tie-dye-shirt
Listen to the soft barbed wire pulling your every limb
Inevitably exploding beyond the rim
See your soul flicker deep in your bones
Every screech making the Purgatory crumble, evermore alone
Sense now your faith engraved on your every cell
Reading that you're the diming ring of a bell.

I love

Boys
Oh god, yes
Boys
With oceans sparkling with golden sunken arcs tucked under chocolate eyes
Girls
Yup, girls
(I'm not gay hon)
Girls who dance like a willow tree and stand like a sycamore
And anyone else who's not societally clean
With bones and scrolls sealed into their pink squishy brains
Bubs, bathtubs, and roofs are my air bubbles
Words, written, sung, and played, are my hallucinogens
Queers' well and maps that breathe down my quivering neck at midnight are my 'borrowed' rafts
Oh, and don't forget the sting that makes me shiver
Red, hot, twisted and bent skin draws angles like honey draws flies
Molten poison that makes my throat erupt like the aurora Polaris
And Oreos, my mamá's homemade Mexican meatballs, her arroz, and pan dulce with a large cool glass of milk

                    I take them like shots with a parched scarred tongue
The safety of the longest kitchen knife giggling under the couch's cushion
as I'm home alone and bullets dance above my head like a halo made of sins
                                Cozy then I can lay on the brown couch
            and stare at a ceiling I can never be with my zit smeared skin
                                El holor de la agua bendita, agua sana
                        Puedes oler la puridad de los gérmenes viejos
                                Flowing in my atheist cupped hands
Stolen silver buried with virgin gods that I only know crumbs of stories of
                                                    Oh god
                                      I'm gonna die alone
                      Because magic is a sin that I'm drowning to kiss.

Writing Activity

1. Diego bravely confronted the fact he had to deal with mental illness. He heals through his writing. You can do it too. What makes you sad? What makes you happy? Write a poem whose first line is what makes you sad and the second line is what makes you happy; how do you get from sad to happy, then?

2. Diego's poems feature several things that make Diego, Diego, such as his Catholic, Mexican-American, and Queer identity. What are parts of your identity? How do they make you, you? Write a poem that highlights those things that make who you are as a person.

3. Diego's poems use beautiful and vivid metaphors. A metaphor is a figure of speech when one thing is made to resemble another thing ex. love is a battlefield, the world is an orange, or Diego's "magic is a sin that I'm drowning to kiss." Write five metaphors and write a poem that uses all five.

Maricarmen Velazquez

Maricarmen Velazquez was born on a rainy, cold day on February 1, 1998 in Houston, TX. The first thing her eyes opened to were her birthgiver's beautiful brown eyes. She is currently seventeen years old. She is also a senior at Stephen F. Austin High School. The relationship she has with her mother, father, and three siblings is very outgoing. Maricarmen plans to attend the University of Houston where she intends to major in Elementary Education; her career aspiration is to become an Elementary School Teacher.

The Pencil

As the pencil, I am being moved across the lines
The lines that create stories, memories and moments
Those stories, memories and moments can cause me
to continue to move across the lines
As I continue to move I stumble upon a problem
A problem that grows in my woodened body
This problem is fear
Yes, I do have an eraser, but there are things that I cannot erase
I fear the sharpener
If I ever encounter the sharpener I will be sharpened
This will make me smaller and weaker
But as the pencil I am excited and looking forward to
writing on new sheets and new lines
For I am the pencil!

Frutero

Mi familia es como una canasta de frutas
Todas las frutas tienen su personalidad
Mi madre es como un montón de uvas,
con su dulcera nos mantiene juntos y unidos

Mi padre es como una papaya,
fuerte por afuera pero dulce por dentro
Mi hermana, Jennifer, es como una pera,
verde por fuera pero blanca y pura por dentro

Mi hermano, Sebastian, es como unas fresas,
que me llena con sorpresas y risas
Mi hermano mayor, Francisco, es como un kiwi,
dulce y agrio a la vez aunque a veces es difícil de entender
Si los conoces bien, seria más fácil comprender

Writing Activity

1. What is your earliest memory, as far back as you can remember? What's so striking about it? Write a story of that memory. Describe everything as accurately as you can.

2. What object do you identify most with? What about you do you see yourself in that object? Write a poem about what that object shares most with you.

3. Now, what about your family? What would you compare your family to? Fruits? Animals? Items? Write a poem about how each member of your family shares attributes with your comparison.

Lizeth Hilario Echeverria

Lizeth Hilario Echeverria was born on October 22, 2001. She is a freshman at Santiago High School in the Garden Grove, California. She lives with her father, mother and older sister. She also has another older sister and older brother living in Mexico. Growing up she never thought life would be so harsh in a misunderstood world. She saw how her sister struggles a lot in life. She noticed life isn't perfect as she thought it was everyday Lizeth was growing and seeing what life really is. As Lizeth grew she always followed the steps of her older sister. This young lady had her sister every day. She had to let her go and go through life by herself. Her sister was going to college, so now she is on her own. She still maintained on following her sisters steps. She had goals on going to college. She began to be more outgoing and started volunteering, becoming herself. When she gets lost some where she doesn't give up she continues and keeps going.

The Beauty of the Sunset

The last time I saw the sunset
I finished my race
I looked up
And saw the sunset
It was beautiful

The colors were orange, yellow and red

As I looked up
I felt the rain drops falling on my face
The breeze blowing through my hair

As I was going home
I thought that it would be my last race
I decided it would not be my last race
I wanted to continue running
And not listen to anyone
Who was trying to keep me down?

I noticed that by seeing the sunset
It made me realize, running is my passion
I would push myself and my limits
To overcome any obstacle in running
This shapes me
It's who I am

What You See

Look into my eyes
Tell me what you see
Tell me what you think of me
What am I, to you?

I am not just a girl
I am a young lady who has grown
From being that little girl
I'm learning about life
Exchanging my dolls for books

So tell me what you see
And what you think of me
I am not just a girl

Writing Activity

1. What advice would you give a youth who is about to enter high school as a freshman. Is there something you would do different? A sport you recommend that helped you cope with the surroundings around you.

2. Discuss in a group in moments that you have felt misunderstood by your friend, family member, or school staff. Do you feel there are imaginary barriers that hold you back from accomplishing your goal's that are due to the misunderstandings you encounter.

3. Think about a moment in which someone did something nice for you that made you feel good inside and inspired to return the favor to someone else. Write down each detail, from how you felt before that person impacted your life to how it felt to help someone else.

Eligio Cisneros

Eligio "Eli" Cisneros was born on January 20, 1998 in Houston, TX. He is the youngest of three brothers and was raised in the East End area, or Second Ward as they call it. Eli rides his bicycle to work, school, college, buy the groceries, and pay the bills, etc. Ever since his father passed away and his brothers moved on with their lives, he has taken it upon himself to look after the well-being of his mother due to her illness. He spends his free time by being the drum major at the Marching band in his high school and interacting with the community. Eli's inspiration comes from his misfortunes and accomplishments. He is currently a senior and has aspirations to become a Chemical Engineer.

The Symbol

The wolf is an animal that hunts for food four times its size, such as the caribou or bison, capable of running for long periods of time driven by hunger or the fear of death. The wolf is an animal capable of sacrificing its own life in order to protect his own offspring or pack. An animal that runs to mom because the hunter is after him. An animal who cries in the night at the tallest hill because his brother died after the bear attacked him. As the wolf cries in anguish, the wolf begins to develop the want of survival. To provide his family with a pinch of happiness because food has ran out. The determined wolf hunts for game but his mom perishes in pain because she is very ill. Every evening the wolf comes back with a spirit of failure under the phase of obscurity since he is deaf from his right ear and has poor eyesight. Thus, he cannot capture game that will satisfy his mother hunger. Then one day the wolf runs and runs because a bear that is chasing him killed his mother for she was too weak to defend herself. The wolf is slowly dying due to starvation. A pack of wolves confront the bear and avenge the death of his brothers and mother. The wolf continues to run to the man in the sky.

Writing Activity

1. Who is someone you care for? As in, who is someone you take time out of your day for or spend energy you could use doing something else to see or visit or talk to? Why?

2. What is something you invest yourself in? It can be a club or activity or hobby or etc. What does that say about you?

3. What animal most closely resembles you? What about yourself do you see in them? Write a day in your life as that animal or write a day in their life as you.

Marcelo Martinez

Marcelo Martinez was born in San Luis Potosi in a little Rancho, La Duana. At the age of five, he migrated to the U.S. because his parents wanted to give him a better future. He took advantage of the opportunity that his parents gave him by overcoming the language barrier, then later became an outstanding student. Marcelo was also involved in programs such as The Academic Achievers Program and Emerging Latino Leaders. He is also pursuing his life time goal of becoming a Civil Engineer.

El Rio Grande

El Rio Grande is the path way to the American Dream.
But is the American Dream really worth you risking your life?
Do you know what the American Dream really is and what it demands?
In Mexico you cultivate your own vegetables and fruit and you live off of them.
But
In the U.S. you come to work every day and you get paid the minimum
But even if you do the hardest work while working every day
sometimes that is not enough for the bill,
the rent and money to support your family in Mexico.
What is the American Dream?

Writing Activity

1. Change can be scary and cost a part of ourselves for the better. What have you done to make your life better? What change did you have to make? Why? Write a poem about the process of that change.

2. "What is the American Dream?" Have you heard of it? How has it been defined? What does the term mean to you? Do they clash or go against each other? Write a poem about how.

3. What place means a lot to you? Write a description of that place. Then write about what that place means to you.

Erick Romero Chavez

Erick Romero Chavez is a 17-year-old teenager that was born and raised in Houston, TX. He had a little sister and they both lived with, and were raised by, their single mother. At first his mother would work and have time to take care of her children, but as timed passed things got more expensive. She had to spend more time at work. It got so bad to a point where she wouldn't even be able to take care of Erick and his little sister. That's how Erick and his sister began to live with family members instead of living with their mom. It was ok because even then Erick's mom would still find time to see them. She didn't work on the weekends so Erick and his sister would go with their mom on the weekend. When he was still a child he would occupy himself with video games. He couldn't get enough of them so his mom decided to put her foot down and say enough is enough. She signed him up for soccer which he ended up enjoying, leading him to play more sports. Once he got a taste of the others he couldn't stop playing. Now he is pursuing his dream of becoming a professional athlete. Sports are what inspire and motivate him to strive and improve in every single way possible.

I am me

I am me
I am my own person
I am the captain of me, not you

I am not a chess piece that can be moved with a fingertip
I am not a tamed horse, I am a mustang
I am a leader, not a follower
I am not a trend follower, I am a trend starter
I am my own man,
No one tells me what to do (except my mother) #lachancla
Notice how I don't rhyme any words
I didn't use enormous words in this poem
Not because I couldn't think of any off the top of my head (which is true)
But also because I don't want to
I decide what goes in this poem
Not you, not your dad, not your mom, not even my own mom
(don't tell her that I just said that) only me.
And if you don't like it then deal with it because...
I am me.

Writing Activity

1. Which people in your life invest in you? As in, who takes time out of their day or spends energy they could've used doing something else to see or talk to you? How so? How does it make you feel?

2. What do you want to do with your life? How did you come to this realization? If you don't have a direction, then what makes you happy now? What would life look like if you can do that for the rest of your life?

3. What makes you, you? How do you define yourself? In what ways? Who tries to define you? Write a poem about how you define yourself.

Rosie Lawyer

Rosie Lawyer is a Pisces born on March 13, 2001 and is the oldest of three. I am 14 years old and will be entering as a freshman at Valley High School in the fall of 2015. I live in a house with other people. I know how to play five instruments but my goal is to play twelve instruments in total. I love the sound and it fulfills me. It is what I will always need in my life. I am undecided for the future but it will come soon.

Who Am I

Perfection is a disease of a nation
yet I still chase it
living in a fairytale
life is tragic

I found out in life
there's no escape from reality
Life has just begun
I'm coiled up on the dirty ground

Now I know that this is life
pain is just the compromise
Thinking you can leave me to die
Was it all a lie?

I used to being happy and filled
with smiles
Now it's all changed

Now I'm looking at the mirror
Disliking what I see
Thinking I can't reach the definition of perfection
That is when it hit me
It is not real, none of it is
If I cant hold it or see it
Then it doesn't exist
None of this matters I have to admit

So now onto my new life
Whatever that may be
Hopefully a life that will suit me

Writing Activity
1. What is your career goal? Plan it out from 1 year to 5 years and revisit your plan. What will be the next steps to get you to where you want to be?

2. Discuss with your group all the possibilities after life and death and write a collective fictional piece about all the scenarios your group came out with using fictional characters.

Karla Moreno

Karla Moreno is a nineteen-year-old, Mexican-American, young woman born July 21, 1995 in Houston, Texas to an amazing woman, Candelaria Reyes, and man, Fidencio Moreno. Karla is first generation born from immigrant parents in the United States and one of the first kids in the family to attend public school in the U.S. without knowing any English, only speaking Spanish. She learned English until the fourth grade and even then, school was difficult because of the language barrier. Finally on June 9, 2013 she walked across the stage at Reliant Stadium to receive her diploma and graduated in the top ten percent of her high school class. She is the first person in her family to go beyond a high school education. As of now, she is attending the University of Houston and is also a member of the Mexican American Studies Student Organization (MASSO).

Le Quiero Decir

In the shadows of the night I cry myself to sleep
Hidden under her manto no quiero salir
I cry and cry and cry, vuelvo a llorar

Le temo a todo no solo a ti
Is this nasty desire que traigo entre mi
Lo siento, lo veo y lo vuelvo a sentir

El ardor que quema todo en mí
No es de Dios is solo a sin

Hidden under her manto no quiero salir
Pues esque si lo hago no quiero destruir
Esa linda imagen que tienes de mí
Yo soy tu niña perfecta your porcelain doll

Y esque mira, deja te cuento que el ser yo no es nada fácil
Soy de color
Soy mujer
Soy Mexicana y a la vez Americana
Pero es que eso no es lo feo no es el mal
Para ti el ser bisexual is the worst sin of all

Te quiero gritar y te quiero decir
Pero salir de este poso no es nada fácil
I tried it once pero en depression caíste
My wrist cried out this beautiful sea of red yet it wasn't enough

I don't know what to say ya no se que decir

Writing Activity

1. What are you afraid to say but can't because you're scared you'll be judged? Write a poem, inspired by Karla's, where you start off accepting who you are and explain why you're scared to tell anyone your secret. You don't have to share this with anyone.

2. Discussion: Why do you think the person in the poem feels this way about accepting who they are? What kind of society/surrounding would drive this person to hurt themselves like this?

3. What identities do you consider yourself? Karla's poem explores Mexican, American, Mexican-American, bisexual, etc. identities and how it is to exist with all of them at once. Make a list and find connections and/or contradictions. How do you feel about this? How do you navigate all these identities?

Jacob Paul Castillo

On April 27, 1998, a baby boy, 11 pounds and 3 ounces, was born at Saint Joseph Hospital. During the labor process, the woman who was having me died, and stated that when she was dead, she was in a white room, a room similar to the one in *Bruce Almighty*, where Jim Carrey and Morgan Freeman were talking in. However, she came back to life soon. My dad has always had a job ever since he was sixteen. There were times where he had been fired or had to look for a new job. But every time that would happen to him, he would quickly find a new job. My dad has always told me to go to college, and always helped me as best as he could in my academic life. My number one goal in life is to help people. I want to go to college and start up my own gun company and make hundreds of thousands of dollars to help others. I want to get families from third-world countries and bring them to America to offer them a chance to get educated. In the city of Houston, the city I was born in, when someone dies, the city doesn't pay for it; the family of the deceased has to pay for it. What I want to do is pay for the funerals for those families who can't afford it. So say a worker on a construction site dies while on duty doing his job, I would pay for his or hers funeral. However, if someone shot up a school and killed themselves during the process, I would not pay for their funeral. I find people so interesting, and I want to help them all. I will end this bio with a quote from my favorite artist. "That time will come, one day you'll see, when we can all be friends" —Freddie Mercury.

It's A Hard Life

I love and hate people.
People are like movies,
Some are better than the others,
And some may make you cry.
But regardless, I want to help them all.

I see myself as an artist,
I am willing to do and try new things,
Willing to give everyone a chance at something,
Willing to take that step that no one else will take,
Having the desire to make things better,
And help those in need.
I want to do amazing things with my life,
And change so many others.

<u>**Writing Activity**</u>
1. Who is your favorite artist/idol? Look up a quote they've either said or wrote in a song/poem/interview/etc. How does it make you feel? Write a response to them by applying that quote to your life.

2. Jacob demonstrates many of his values here, such as helping those in need. What are some values you live by? Why? Write a story of when your values were needed most from another person.

3. What is a hard life? Do you know anyone who has had one? Write a story or poem about that person and what makes their life hard. How can it get better?

Vanessa Marcos

Vanessa Marcos is an outgoing Chicana. She is a 13-year-old that was born in Tustin but raised in Santa Ana, California. She lives with her two sisters, one brother, and her two parents. Her favorite things to do are play videogames, swim, ride her bike, play basketball, and also protest. She protests because she wants to ensure equal rights to everyone and also to stop police brutality. Her goals are going to high school and graduating high school. She also wants to go and graduate from college and become a doctor.

Community

I think we can inform the community by making news. We can make peaceful protest. We too stop the community from seeing the bullshit they put on news. We have to organize as a community. We have to inform our people of our struggle. If they see someone get pulled over just watch to make sure the cops don't abuse their power. Remember, if they didn't have a badge or a gun they would be nothing but people. Look at the government, do you see anybody looking to make a change to your city or country. All I see is cops killing people letting them die. Remember that the government, police, school cops, and teachers can't bring you down just because of your culture or color.

Dear Community

"You build a fence, we climb a fence", it's funny how these non-colored people are trying to keep us away from our homeland. They only believe in the government to help them out and they are always against our community. While we colored people are being killed and incarcerated by non-colored people. The only protection we have are each other because we are community. We need no police or government because all they are doing to us is killing our own and keeping us poor. I have never seen a rich white person get killed by a police. Recently, I heard a white man who shot up a church full of colored people. He got arrested, however police said he had a mental problem and took him to get help. If it were someone of color the police wouldn't even hesitate to shoot him or her.
Yours truly,
Vanessa

Writing Activity

1. Name the various types of problems that exist in our society. Create a visual with your group.

2. Why is history so important in school? How does "history repeat itself"? Provide specific examples.

3. Vanessa Marcos is a young activist whom uses her voice as her weapon to express how she feels. Are you involved in a local group in your community that fights for a social justice issue and how has your involvement created an impact on you? Write a letter like Vanessa's piece, "Dear Community" and what would you want to tell your community about what you see and how to fight the issues in your neighborhood.

Karina Mendez

Karina Mendez was born on February 4, 1998 and raised in Houston, TX. She's currently seventeen-years-old and a senior at Stephen F. Austin High School. Karina plans on attending the University of Houston and go into the medical field. She also believes that hard work and the effort you put into what you desire is the key to success.

About Me

Karina,
Shy, funny, loving and caring,
Sister of Jesus, Jose and Grecia,
Lover of food, sleep and dogs,
Who feels joy when shopping, exercising and listening to music,
Who needs her family, friends and attention,
Who gives love, laughter and help,
Who fears growing old, failure and losing her parents,
And who would like to see success, make her parents proud, and a better world.

Mi Familia

Para mí, la familia es los más puro e importante en la vida. Tengo una madre y un padre que son muy trabajadores, cariñosos y protectores. Que me han dado mucho más de lo que necesito y que sé que lo harán haciendo hasta que ya no puedan más. ¿Mi "ama?" Es una mujer trabajadora y ama de casa a la vez, una cariñosa madre y buena esposa. La primera y mejor amiga que siempre eh tenido y que me guiara al camino correcto. ¿Mi "apa?" Es un hombre muy trabajador, cariñoso y fuerte que siempre ha hecho lo posible por sacar a mi familia y a mí adelante. Tengo un hermano mayor llamado Jesus, después sigo yo y por ultimo serían los más pequeños Jose y Grecia. ¿Bueno Jesus? Es el mayor de los cuatro que siempre se asegura der ser el buen ejemplo, a veces enojón pero más que nada es mi mejor amigo, que siempre me ayuda y aconseja para ser mejor. Mientras que Jose y Grecia son unos pequeños rebeldes, cariñosos y niños con muchas locas ocurrencias. Esta es mi familia… Que al pesar de las dificultades que hemos pasado juntos siempre encontramos el camino correcto para seguir adelante como familia.

Writing Activity
1. How would you describe yourself? Write a poem about you. This can help you get started: write down five nouns (person, place, or thing) and your relation to them. Write down five emotions (anger, sadness, happiness, etc.) and what makes you feel them? Write down five adjectives (words that describe things, such as strong, big, small, loud, etc.) and how they describe you.

2. Who do you consider your family? Family doesn't have to be blood related, just people in your life who help and support you. Describe them and why they are your family.

3. What nicknames do you have for people, places, or things? Why do you use that nickname? Write a poem where the title is the nickname and the poem is why that nickname exists. The poem may reveal something about you.

Elizabeth Marcos

Elizabeth Marcos was born in Santa Ana, California on January 7, 1998. She is a 17-year-old young lady who wants to become a speech pathologist and help those who face the difficulty of speaking and not being able to express themselves. She wants to receive her Master's Degree from Ohio State University.

She lives with her two loving, hardworking parents, her outspoken brother, and two beautiful young sisters. Elizabeth is currently enrolled at Saddleback High School as a senior. She is part of AVID and Upward Bound which are college readiness programs that help her prepare for her transitioning from high school to college. She is trying her hardest in school to achieve her aspiration which is to be able to pay off her home to help her parents out. Outside of school, she enjoys swimming, football, water polo and tutors youth. She wants to make a change for youth who have a difficult time in school and at home. That's her biggest dream and believes she will achieve that and much, much more.

Hijas

Running up and down the stairs
Racing my sister up to the third floor of the apartments
Biting, punching
Pulling each other's hair to get first place
Scraping ourselves against the light brown rocky walls

Running to the light blue rails where we would stick out our feet
Getting home and running to the balcony to jump onto our little Barbie car
To drive it through the third floor
Ladies would start yelling out the white windows
"Niñas, aqui no se juega!"
Yes, that was home!
My mother yelling
"Hijas a comer!"
My little sisters and I would rush
Accidentally stepping on the little pink Barbie jeep just to get to the hallway
You can smell the delicious scent of frijoles and mole poblano

Writing Activity

1. What is your earliest childhood memory? Narrate a memory most meaningful like in Elizabeth's "Hijas" writing piece. What did it smell like? Who were there?

2. Did you know not all countries offer free education? As a research project, identify the countries in which education is provided for free from elementary to university—for all socioeconomic backgrounds. Then create a list of all the countries that don't. Share what you find.

Jesse Castillo

I am a hard working Mexican trying to not end up on the corner of a liquor store, I have had trouble with the law and school and my only escape is poetry, I hope some people can relate to my poetry and I might be able to influence them, I think the best way to fight oppression is with words.

RED STREETS

My peoples blood stains the road, clips dump out of automatics to reload, to relocate and control power of drugs army's and booze, realize you're going to lose fighting prejudice and dominant police and white supremacy still on the front line looking into the eyes of all my enemies, I feel like OJ when I step into the car cops always in the review my point is to realize the power of oppression its worth addressing that cop tactics don't work on poetry handcuffs or arresting.

RAIN

Rain comes every now and then, washing away the day before the blood of solders brings the tide to shore, the needles for heroin flushed down the drainpipe, washes away the hype from the other days gang fight, washes away all the sweat and tears, tomorrow is a new day with no need for fear.

Writing Activity

1. Do you sometimes find yourself thinking to yourself random thoughts all at once, without pauses and images are quite detailed in your mind, like flashes of moments? Describe aloud one of those moments in 3 sentences or less.

2. Jesse's prose poetry is like flashes of vivid moments and ideas in his mind. Using Jesse's work as an example and your own flashes of moments and ideas, create a collection of random thoughts, remember to use descriptions and emotions. Shoot for three different ones, then title them!

   Prose poetry is poetry written in **prose** instead of using verse but preserving poetic qualities such as intensified imagery, parataxis (the placing of phrases one after another without matching) and emotional effects.

Joana Tello

My name is Joana Tello. I was born in Houston, TX on October 12, 1996, or "Día de la Raza" you will call it. "The Day of the Race." I live with my two loving parents, my brother, and sister. I am the youngest out of the tree. I attend Austin High School where I am currently a senior.

MACHISTAS

Men are so MACHISTAS. Siempre burlándose de las mujeres. That they don't know how to drive. Que no servimos para nada. But they never look at what they do. Ellos nunca miran las cosas que ellos hacen mal. Siempre burlándose de la mujer. "NO QUE MI VIEJA NO SIRVE PA NADA." Si mujeres ellos son Machistas. Yes ladies they are MACHOS. They feel that they can boss us around. But today we are going to say NO!!!!! Mujeres no se dejen de los hombres. Don't let them treat us like dogs. Si te queda el saco, póntelo!!!

Writing Activity
1. Joana confronts 'machismo,' aggressive masculine pride that believes men are better than women. Does Joana agree? Do you agree? Write a response to 'machismo' about what you think about this, drawing inspiration from Joana's piece.

2. Joana marks her birthday with a moment in history, "El Día de la Raza," or, the day commemorating when Christopher Columbus 'discovered' America. What's your birthday? Use the internet to look up what historically happened on the day you were born. Write a response on what that means to you.

3. There are times in life where we get hurt by people or things, either physically or mentally. Joana bravely writes a letter to 'machismo' where she turns their words into her strength. What or who has hurt you? Write a letter to that person or thing and end on how that has made you a stronger person.

Alfredo Marcos

Alfredo Marcos mostly known as "Freddy" is a Mexican-American teenager born in Santa Ana California on September 20th 1999. Freddy was born to a mother and a father and has an older brother and sister. Freddy enjoys writing short fiction stories and once he heard about Barrio Writers, he decided to join. Freddy being a new member to Barrio Writers, hopes to have his stories and writings published. He is hoping to graduate high school and go to UCLA. Freddy's dream is to become a father someday because he always looks up to his father. Freddy aspires to become a counselor to help people in their time of need.

Dear Police

They call themselves "heroes", we call them criminals. Police brutality seems to keep on being a problem for our society. Most of the police officers we seemed to know and love are killing innocent people. Who do we call when the police officers are the killers? I used to feel safe knowing that if anything dangerous ever happens that I have the police to call. Lately, that all has changed. All I have is my community to feel safe from those killers. We all do everything we can do to stop police brutality such as forming riots and protest but they still kill. The cops don't just kill but they discriminate. All the cops are doing are just judging us by our race. The more and more police do this the more people will finally start opening their eyes and figure out that we are not the ones that started this fight. I just fear that this will take a very long time. As communities we will all gather in one voice and to let that cops know that they are the ones who made the wrong choice. Justice will be served for the lives that we lost in the hands of the police and we can all finally live as a society in peace.

Writing Activity

1. What are some issues your community is facing at the moment? Has your community and/or culture been effected by police brutality? If so, what is the community doing to have their opinions heard by the local police and city council?

   Police Brutality is the use of excessive force, usually physical, carried out by local law enforcement activities which includes verbal attacks and physiological intimidation.

2. As a class, discuss 3 ways you, as an individual and a group, can help alleviate one of the problems in your community.

Midnight Amber Smith

My name is Midnight Amber Smith. I was born in San Augustine, Texas in May 19, 2001. I am a freshman. My family is Kim Harries, my mom, my dad is Tommy Harries. My siblings are Antwone Smith and Destiny Smith. I am what you call a country, hip hop, anime bookworm. I am the kind of person who would sit down in a cool shaded area reading a book. This story that I am about tell you is about what kind of person I hope to be.

A look in my life

Past: I was somewhat a quiet kid, you would have thought I was not ever there. They thought I was shy at first but as time grew by their thought went from shy to mute. I knew I could not stay quiet forever, I have to talk to them or they would use sign language to talk to me! I was so scared to talk to anyone. I would let others talk first and watch. I knew I had to speak, I just had to talk. I thought would they laugh at me, was I too weird or was it they thought I was too stuck up to talk to them. I had to swallow my fear and face the truth, I needed to talk!

Present: I am here because I want to make a difference in life. What can I do if I just sit back and let life pass me? Nothing at all. I was no coward. I will tell you that I may not be a big person in the world, but I can help make a difference in it. There are other teens out there waiting to be heard. I would like to help them get their voices out there. "We stand united, one for all and all for one." See who you stand by. Will your so called "friends" help you or drag you down to the bottom? Ask yourself, "Will you fade away or will you make history?" I know I made my choice. How about you, what will you do next? Will you stand by the people who will help you rise to the top or the people who will drag you down? Choose wise because it can change your life for better or worst.

Thank you for listening to my story, now make your own story and rise to the top.

Writing Activity
1. How would you describe your 'Past' and 'Present'? Have you changed in the last 5 or ten years? How so?

2. Where do you see yourself 5 or even 10 years from now? Not just school or career wise but personality wise too…what type of adult/leader do you want to be?

3. Now like Midnight Amber, write your past, present and also include your future!

Monica Hernandez

Monica Hernandez, 17 years, is fascinated with the arts of her culture. A fierce soccer player thirsty to learn all she can about the latino/a, chicano/a studies. She's a dancer, singer, dreamer, and writer. Passionately strolling through life enjoying experiences, cherishing her jumbo size family with eyes wide open.

Rosario

I lay in my bed with content
knowing me and my family are healthy and wise
and together.
This is what I know.
This is all I know.
and it is up to me to engrave it
to my little ones tambien. A healthy body leads to a healthy mind
"Your body is your temple mija, love it
and take care of it."

I lay here thinking of my hijo's face
when I told him about his great grandpa Pete
and all his crazy adventures with his 13 kids.
I'm grinning at my flashback to this morning

taking a glimpse at my kids
in the rearview mirror
on our way to the catholic church
"Padre, hijo, spiritu, santo chicos!"
I teach my kids to love God
and what it's like to be loved by him

I lay here chuckling at the memory of my nina
helping her tio cook
at our weekly bar-be-que catch up de la familia
I teach my kids the rich importance
of a close family
and our blood
our culture
and lifestyles

I can't control what happens
when they grow up
and leave
in all my goodness
Im showing them
how to love
and appreciate all they are

Before I go to sleep
I close my eyes with content
passing on all my heart
Oh, how my abuelo
and abuela
are so proud
smiling down from heaven above.

Howdy

To live in Latexo means
Go out into the world to see white people
"Howdy baby, how are youuuuu?"
the jacked up 2015 trucks in the high school parking lot
fear and burden of going to Walmart and seeing

EVERYBODY you know and their mama
The unaccepting girls from second grade
The pervish old white man from work who winks
when you walk by
The seemingly endless pastures and giant pecan trees
and pinos
vast dark skies at night
with the bright estrellas hanging
I love it
I hate it

Writing Activity

1. The idea of the body as a temple, expressed by Monica in her first poem, is a popular idea. The Xicana feminist writer and teacher Cherrie Moraga asks the question "What does the body know?" referring to the ancestral and cultural knowledge of the body, passed down through the generations.

   Consider what you may have inherited from your family. What rituals and traditions do you instinctually know because of them? Write a poem that expresses this knowledge.

2. What legacy do you hope to leave behind for the future generations of your family? Write a poem or prose response that expresses those hopes.

3. Many of us have a love/hate relationship with our town, especially if it is small, where everyone knows everyone. Read or listen to Tim Hernandez's poem "Home." How does he use a developing image to represent his town, and how does this image reflect how he feels about Fresno? How does Monica do the same in her poem? Write a poem that expresses your hometown and how you feel about in one or a series of sensory images.

John Anthony Muñoz

My name is John Anthony Muñoz, already 18 years old. I was born in Houston, TX. Two strong ladies raised me because my dad was a weak person that couldn't help me. I am proud to be a Hispanic that was raised by two women through rough times. I enjoy playing basketball and listening to music. I love electronic music. It makes me daze out and think about different things that are happening. My goals are to graduate school and college to have a professional career in the business world and have a big house. I've had many accomplishments, mostly from sports and for having perfect attendance and honor roll. There have been a lot of obstacles I overcame to get to where I am. I faced a time where my mother's didn't have enough money for my equipment. My sport was soccer and I would train hard to earn a spot in the varsity team. My main problem was that I didn't have money to pay for my physical and for other equipment that was needed. Coaches would see that I was interested in playing soccer for the school. Putting work in was the best thing to do because at the end I earned an award that I could be recognized with. Coaches would also let me borrow equipment in order for me to be a success in the sport of soccer. Now I have many other goals to pursue and achieve.

About Me

The best thing in the world and the best stress reliever is playing any sport. All kinds of sports are greatly enforced with being physically strong while including activities that bring all kinds of people (short, tall, chubby, skinny, and people from a different race) together.

My favorite sport is playing basketball. I have a passion for it because it helps me release all the things that are going wrong. Each day I get the chance to play I feel like a completely different person who is focused on reaching his goal of being a professional basketball player and become one of the greatest of all time. Playing basketball is amazing because I gain communication and participation skills, which help me be more social with people. I also get to know and make more friends.

I am physically strong with a bunch of problems behind a big smile.

Writing Activity

1. What are some obstacles you've faced in your life? How did you overcome them? Who helped you? Write a story about how a community came together to help you, or how you became part of a community to help others.

2. What clubs or groups are you a part of? Why are you part of them? What do they mean to you? Write a response about how that group defines you, perhaps talking about an event or a person from that club or group.

3. How do you relieve stress? Why does it work for you? Write a poem where the first half is about what stresses you out, then the second half about how you relieve that stress.

Darlene Ayala

Darlene Ayala was born in Orange County, CA on January 13 1998. Her family is a well rounded family who always spend time together. Darlene loves her baby sister named Camila. Darlene goes to Valley High School where she is going to be a senior (Class of 2016). She is the advance dance captain and is on the wrestling team. She is 17 years old and hopes to study Criminal Justice and get her CPE in Accounting. Darlene in the past has struggled with writing and reading but gives thanks to her dad as every holiday break Darlene's dad would make her write essays that helped her descriptive writing. Darlene currently lives in Santa Ana, CA and hopes to achieve her goals.

My Mistakes

I HEAR ANGELS
MY GRANDMA SAID
I SPOKE WITH CONFIDENCE AS I LAY IN BED
THE SINS CAME AND I GAVE IN
ADAM AND EVE
WERE MY ESCAPE
I TOOK THE APPLE AND I SAID AMEN
BEFORE YOU I KNEELED

BEFORE YOU I HAVE LED MY ESCAPE
CAN YOU FORGIVE ME I SAID
I WAS HURT
I WAS IN PAIN
AND IN YOUR ARMS YOU WAIT
ONE LAST TIME I HEARD THE ANGELS
I SLEPT UNDERNEATH MY BED OF DEATH
WITH MY EYES SHUT I LISTEN TO THE CRIES I HAVE SUNG

Breath to Death

Breathing, gasping under the same human flesh
Hope is dead, but the hope of the last piece of hair
Is underneath the one thing keeping you standing
White pale skin, and the crease under the unreplaceable bags
Under the only thing that keeps you from watching yourself from your death bed
Death is unexpected but the light that fights to keep it on
Is a few seconds or instant far apart from life
The last thing before your death is your breath
Cherish the very breath that can become your last moment
The for white walls become the home of your soul
Trembling next to the one noise
That is knowing you're alive or just another waste of space
With the rest of unknown souls

Unexplained

she pushed … i came
She ran ….i followed
You left ….i wondered
you called… i denied
your threats … i cried
years followed …i grew
she reached … i pushed

years pass
i pushed ...she never came
she never loved...i never learned to love

Society

Society?
We turn brutality to make us one
Hear the police car
And suddenly we all start to adjust as one
Don't let a cause make us one
Unite us to enforce
Don't use your choice
Us what's right
Abuse isn't to unite us as a society
It's to fight as one
And to tell the scars that are left behind our bloody carved backs
So write
Read
Speak
We all get the point
We all have to stand up
And praise to your own choice
So fight the cause
But as what you believe in

Writing Activity
1. Has an event in your life ever changed your emotions for a long period of time? How did you deal with the emotions?

2. What type of "freewriting" do you do? How does it help you think clearer and get to the final idea?

   Freewriting: often done on a daily basis as part of the writer's daily routine, usually for 5, 10, or 15 minutes. Write without worrying about grammar, spelling, or making corrections (revisions or editing). It's one way to reduce writer's block and develop a natural voice. If you reach a point where you can't think of anything to write, then write that you can't think anything, until something you think of something else to write.

Jenna Abshire

Jenna Abshire is a 17 year-old high school student in her senior year. She was born April 28, 1998 in Fresno, California, but moved to Texas with her family when she was two. Currently living in Austin, she spends her time playing roller derby with TXJRD as their captain, and working at a dog ranch. In her future, Jenna plans to go to college, continue playing derby, eventually start up and train her own junior derby team, and continue writing, hopefully leading her to join CantoMundo.

Selfish (self-ish)

Adjective
1. (of a person, action, or motive) lacking consideration for others; concerned chiefly with one's own personal profit or pleasure

I am selfish
I am selfish because I'm dedicated to a sport I love

I am selfish because I want to see my boyfriend more than once a week, because just a few weeks ago I almost lost him forever

I am selfish because I'm trying to do things
and go places on my ownwithout my friends or family

Because I'm trying to open myself up and grow as a person
I am selfish because these people will not be around in a year,
so I'm trying to get used to being without them, to being okay without them

I am selfish because sometimes I want to be left alone
I am selfish because sometimes I don't feel like talking
I am selfish because I don't always have good days
I am selfish because sometimes I just feel like crying, for no reason
I am selfish because I have feelings and I want them to be acknowledged for once
I am selfish because I am sensitive
I am selfish because I am powerful
I am selfish because I am a woman
And I will continue to be selfish
I am simply realizing that I matter too

Writing Activity

1. After reading Jenna's poem, discuss if you think she's being selfish or independent. Point out specific lines that make you think one way or another about her "selfishness." Have you ever been called selfish for focusing on yourself?

2. Write a response piece to Jenna's poem. In a response piece, you analyze the writing, but you also include your personal impression. Sometimes it's just something the writing made you think about, a small connection to the words, images and theme. Sometimes you simply change the end of each line, go ahead try it, then edit as you please!

3. When Jenna read this piece at the Barrio Writers Live Reading in Austin summer 2015, she surprised herself, she didn't think she would cry or even present like a slam poet but her true emotions came out. Check out Button Poetry on YouTube, some of our favorites are Amaris Diaz, Kai Davis and Denice Frohman. Website: https://www.youtube.com/user/ButtonPoetry

   Then write your piece, as response (and perform) to anyone you watch on Button Poetry!

Adrian Martinez

I was born in Tustin 2002 October 20th. Four years after I was born my family moved to Santa Ana and went into pre-school. In pre-school I made some really good friends but, I'd get in trouble at certain times. A year later I entered first grade at Martin Luther King Jr. Elementary School. In second grade I transferred to Heroes elementary school where I made new friends. However, in third grade everything changed it was a HORRIBLE experience for me. I was put in the Think Together program, which was basically a program for after school youth and that where I started to get bullied. I was bullied and other kids made some myths for the rest of the third graders that the boys restroom was haunted and me I was actually stupid enough to believe the myth. Sometimes when I go to the restrooms, but sometimes the bully would lock me in the restroom. Every time I would tell the teacher, the teacher wouldn't do anything. In the fourth grade I went to Orange County Educational Arts Academy (OCEAA), and sometimes I would get in trouble. I would get bad grades in math and I went that same school for two more years. I auditioned for International Dance at OCSA and entered in the 7th grade. Now it's August and now I am a Barrio Writer.

Police Troubles

Police don't trust Latinos, Mexicans and African American people because they like to stereotype us thinking we can't do anything about this brutality. The question is why are the police pricks? Why can't they have second thoughts of who we actually are? They put a bullet in our bodies when we try and flee, when all we want is to live.

Writing Activity
1. Define "Stereotypes" and discuss among your group what are some of stereotypes carried on by society that affect how we live every day.

2. Watch Kendrick Lamar's music video, "Alright." How does his song talk about police brutality throughout the different scenes? Kendrick Lamar is from Compton, California and he has openly talked about the issues that his community goes through and his use of hip hop to express himself.

3. Is there a hip hop song that describes some of the issues that your neighborhood is going through? Write a response to that hip hop song and use all your five senses to express the emotions and scenarios.

Jazmin Condado

Yo, I'm Jazmin Condado. I was born in Houston, Texas on July 6th, 2000. My interests include eating (a lot), watching anime, annoying my friends & family, dogs, Vocaloid, and staring at nature. My biggest brag-worthy accomplishments are successfully presenting a 3D Vocaloid hologram at the Don Coleman Coliseum while singing alongside the Texas Medical Center Orchestra at the Wortham Theater and having a GPA of 3.76. I hope to make it to and through college to pursue a degree in law.

A Real Latina

How do you define a Latina? Brown hair? Big thighs? Wide hips? Curvy body? Caramel skin? How do you know? TV shows? Movies? Porn? With that being said, what is a real Latina? Is a real Latina a maid? Is a real Latina pregnant at fifteen? Is a real Latina submissive? Is a real Latina uneducated? Hell no! A real Latina endures every and all conflicts with a strong heart and a bright smile. A real Latina aids her family but does not lose sight of her ambitions unless necessary. A real Latina proves everyone wrong, destroying what society expects for her to be and sets a new exceptional standard. A real Latina sets sky high standards for herself. A real Latina is unbreakable with your stupid stereotypes. A real Latina challenges the world with confidence glistening in her eyes. A real Latina strives to make it to the top and when she cannot, she will inspire her children to make it farther than she ever would. A real Latina will treat herself like the queen she is. A real Latina knows her worth and will not settle for your bullshit. A real Latina takes pride in who she is and where she is from. A real Latina is a devoted mother, aspiring sister, and a productive daughter. So if you, sir, come up asking for a Latina, expecting a curvy and easy young women, then you, sir, do not know what a real Latina looks like.

Writing Activity

1. What are accomplishments you're proud of? Why? Write a poem where each accomplishment starts a line and write why you're proud of them next to them.

2. How do you define yourself? How do others (like movies, TV shows, pornography) define you? What makes you real? How do you defy definitions?

3. What does society want you to be? Is that what you want to be? If so, write a story of what you will be like in your future. If not, write a story of how you will live your life against society's demands. Will you be happy? How?

CJ Sounds

CJ Sounds is a 16-year-old, homosexual, genderfluid student at Lanier High School. In his life, he's had to give up a lot, to leave a lot of things behind. He believes his greatest achievement has been surviving this long in this horrible, horrible world; the only thing keeping him going being his desire to make a name for himself and to leave a mark behind for future generations. In the time of him having to give a lot up to be where he is, his dreams have changed and his morals have been modified, but writing has always been one of those dreams, and will continue to be those dreams in the future.

May
Tuesday
I'm alone. I'm alone, and he's coming over. He's coming over…to my house. I bite my lip, and I try to take my mind off of things. I try to think about how *good* it'll feel. How much *happier* I'll be afterwards.
But of course, I can't.

My mind is plagued with self-doubt and broken-worded thoughts. "What if he changes his mind?" "What if he kidnaps me?" "What if he hurts me?"
My phone rings; I have a text message. Turning to check it… it's from him. He wants me to come outside.

I walk out to the front of the apartment complex and say hi, giving him a hug. He asks me where a corner store is and I immediately think "Oh god, he's gonna kidnap me."

I tell him that it's just down the street, but he quickly mentions while driving over to my place, he saw none. He asks if it would be okay for me to show him.

I'm nervous, anxious with fear. But I say yes. Climbing into his car, I look at him, luckily my blush blends in with my skin. He looks back at me and smiles, placing a comforting hand on my leg, and I lean onto his shoulder, just sitting there before he starts to drive.

I point out each turn with sharp detail, making sure that he misses none of them and I ask, "Are you going to take me back to my place?" He gets a concerned look, and strokes my cheek with his thumb, causing me to lean into his hand for comfort as he nods and places a kiss to my forehead.

Then he walks into the store, and I'm still in the car. I'm now shivering with anxiety, and I'm sure he can notice. When he walks out, he's carrying a 12 pack of beer which he places at my feet, and puts what I assume to be beer salt in a cupholder.

And then we drive back; he remembers the way to my house. One of his hands is on my leg, comforting me and... touching me through the fabric of my pants. I'm less scared. I place soft kisses on his arm and smile, watching him.

We arrive back at my house, and he opens a beer, sprinkling some of the salt on his hand as a garnish. I sit on my bed awkwardly, watching him for a moment before he walks over and starts to kiss me. I'm swept into the heat of the moment; his lips taste *good* against my lips. He climbs onto the bed with me, bumping into a shelf and I laugh, causing him to laugh too. We're covered in sweat, clothes scattered on the floor as we entangle our limbs in each other as our energy dies down. He smiles and kisses my forehead, but he knows he has to leave soon. An hour later, he goes; just as quickly as he came.

Next Thursday
He brought me chocolate; I wanted to eat it off of his body, but he just laughed and kissed me, dismissing the fact.

He's become more passionate; like he feels comfortable with my body... like he knows me. He's not afraid to think outside of the box, he's no longer reserved. We're closer.

I told him I have feelings for him — he thinks we should wait until I get out of high school... I agree.

He compliments me a lot this time, not that he hadn't been doing it before, but I had to make a note of it... it was endearing, almost sweet.

June
Tuesday
There's this burning pain in my backside, and I tell him. He says be strong and it will pass; I trust him.

Friday
The pain has seemed to increase since two days ago; it's hard to walk now. It's like a scorpion stung me in the butt. My mom offers to take me to the hospital and I agree; this pain is unbearable.

I forget to tell him I'm going to the hospital.

Saturday
We take a taxi, and the doctor is afraid it might be herpes, so he collects some samples. He then asks my mom to step out, and, no matter how much her protest, he tells her he has to keep confidentiality. I feel more comfort without her in the room.

I tell him all that has happened; our time together, what we did, and he just nods, a concerned look in his eyes. He says he'll have to tell my mom.

Two weeks later
I don't talk to "him" anymore. I don't have a phone; the police are taking care of things. My mom doesn't trust me. Before my phone was taken, I told him all that I could without directly mentioning law enforcement. I could tell he didn't want to say goodbye based on all the questions he was

asking.

I realize that I love him.

July

School is out, and I am still here; my mother still doesn't trust me, and I am still missing him. He wasn't my first, but he was the most memorable. I asked one of my friends if she could tell him something for me; as she contacts him, he says he doesn't know anyone by my name, age, or location. She comforts me, and I thank her.

And even now, I'm still trying to move on.

Full of Wonder

I have this friend
    For personal reasons,
        He doesn't wish his name to be **revealed.**
In his dreams,
He goes places,
He sees things…

    Things none of us would *ever* dream of.

His dreams are **extravagant.**
                      Spell-binding…
                                    WORLD-shaking.

He says:
He feels like he's
R u n n i n g
against the wind.

    Like He's s w i m m i n g against the current.

He knows what he **should** do…
                But he also knows what he *wants* to do.

And one of these
Holds more personal **satisfaction.**

I watch him doing these things
    And I hope he reaches his goal.
        I hope the **S T A R S** in his eyes never go out.
        I hope he keeps on being…

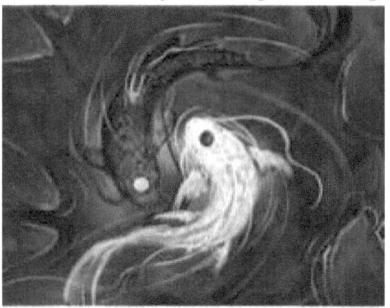

DAZZLING.
    Starry-eyed
        Full of **W O N D E R…**
            Full of *dreams*.
MUTED.
    Weary-eyed
        Full of **p a i n…**
            Full of <u>S O R R O W.</u>

They mix beautifully to create this **never-ending** dance
            That is
life.

Writing Activity
1. In the poem, "Full of Wonder," CJ utilized word art and mixed media to communicate a dreamlike quality. Mixed media is when artists use images, paintings, photos and words together to engage the viewer and communicate an idea. How do these visuals pair with the words to create fuller images? How does the word art emphasize the feelings that CJ wanted to communicate?

Oftentimes, writers use art to inspire them to write, and other times, like CJ, they have an image in mind that they want to use to juxtapose with their words.

CJ got his picture of the koi fish from a visual artist on www.deviantart.com. Explore some of the visual art there and write a poem in response to that image.

2. In the diary entries, the author uses a first person voice to reveal how their relationship with someone changed over time. What does this reveal about how an interaction or event in our lives can change us forever? How does the use of the diary form help the author reveal complicated emotions such as love, desire, and trauma? How do they use this confessional form to reclaim their voice and sense of self?

Confession is the act of revealing something deeply personal that may be embarrassing or painful, especially in writing. This can be the hardest type of writing because it requires the writer to be honest with themselves about their experiences, and reveal their own pain in order to be able to heal.

Think of a friend or someone you know who has revealed something difficult to you. What would you want them to know or how could you support them? Write a list of things you could say that might help them feel safe and accepted.

Sapphire Sea

I was born in Vancouver, Washington but moved to Nacogdoches, Texas with my mom and my sister Ruby. I lived with my mom, dad, and Sister for 13 years until the accident happened.

Where do crows go after morning?
Prologue

Drake lived an okay life with his mother.
His father left upon learning of her pregnancy. It doesn't matter if he was without a dad. The guy didn't deserve Drake's mom anyway. Drake compared the guy to a lizard; it's all chill till something—parenting—tries to catch it.

Drake, the good seed of a bad father. Sometimes he'd wake to his mum crying about how she was a bad parent, but Drake always found a way to calm her down. She would call him her crow, a beauty only Artmetis—the moon goddess—could understand. This would make Drake wonder, where do crows go after morning? Once when he was younger, he asked his mother the question, she replied, "I don't know. Try to find out." He would get the answer to his question of life.

Writing Activity

1. Read Sapphire's prologue. Did it make you want to read more of the story? Why or why not?

    Prologue: *noun*, a separate introductory section of a literary or musical work.

2. Now, think about what would or should come after this prologue. Work in small groups, one group writes one page of the first chapter of the book, then passes it on to the next group, then write the next page and so on (or just work on your own). Keep going, write Sapphire's book!

    Or, write your own prologue to a future story, hurry get started! If you want to write the first chapter, go ahead, turn it into a book! ☺

Chris Sida

Christian Sida was born a shy and quiet boy on January 15, 1999. The first few years he lived with his single mother in Santa Ana, California. Later his mother met a new man that soon became Christian's new father. Growing up Christian witnessed domestic violence between his father and mother. For Christian, this was an opening to new way of expression of feelings through his writing. Growing up in a home with domestic violence between his parents became normal for him. He decided to focus on himself along with his studies. As a hobby, Christian makes and edits music. Throughout his life, music has been his passion. As he entered high school, he had many letters sent to him from colleges to give him courses over the summer. Unfortunately, money was a big thing when it came to it so he put it down. Over the summer, Christian stumbled across the Barrio Writers. He was hesitant to join but then assured himself that this was the place for him, a place to express himself through writing.

One Intersection with Much Culture

The intersection is a constant flow, endless, never stopping.
The sound of honks, the sound of wheels on pavement.
The low-soft music coming from the restaurant, Tacos Tijuana.
The sound of sizzling meat and the smell of fresh vegetables laid out.
The bread that rises in the bakery.

From the smell of the bread, to the sweet aroma from the laundry mat, sounds of the clothes in the dryer. The wishing of the machines and the klink of the coin dispenser.
The crying kids that are afraid to leave their mothers in exchange for 6 hours of education.
The chatters and whispers of teens in high school.
This intersection never dies out, sun coming down and moon popping up is no exception for it to stop.
At night the hounds bark in threat.
The muffled sounds of gunshots could be heard.
The many sounds of sirens getting louder each minute.
All this within one single intersection.

What Type?

What type are you? Are you the type to do drugs, to drop out of school? Are you the type to get pregnant at a young age, or work people's lawn? No you are not. Stereotype after stereotype. You are not a criminal, a thief, a mugger! You are yourself. Not someone who goes by their given stereotype. It's time for you to stop caring on what people say. It's time to raise your voice to show those that you are smart, bright, and intelligent. It's time for you to say that you are above of what people think you are. So tell me, what type are you?

Writing Activity
1. Have you ever felt misunderstood or judged by how you look or speak? How did it make you feel? Did you wish you could change the outcome? Write your own response to Chris Sida's piece, "What Type?"

2. How does your community influence the world around you and help shape your identity?

   Identity: the fact of being who or what a person or thing is.

3. Discuss among your group, Do you like poetry? Why or why not? Did you know hip hop and rap are a form of poetry? Who are your favorite poets/hip hop artists? Why do you like them?

Melanie Elaine Salazar

Melanie Elaine Salazar is a seventeen year old who was born in Houston, Texas from Hispanic parents. She is a very strong believer in that through hard work, dedication, and perseverance, anything can be achieved. Even through hardships and struggles in her life, she has realized that in order to overcome and succeed, she must keep strong and not let any of that put a hold on her future goals and dreams.

Currently, Melanie is at the top of her high school class. She feels the urge to be a positive role model for her society and the future generations. Because of this, she has involved herself in many extracurricular activities that will have a great lasting impact on her future. Some of these extracurricular activities include: the Academic Achievers Program at UH CMAS; the Interact Club from Harrisburg 5890; the National Honor Society; the Science National Honor Society; and being the vice president of her class. These organizations have caused her to gain great leadership skills that will hopefully help her become a great individual in society and influence generations to come.

Her short term goal and dream is to obtain a degree in the engineering field while her long term goal is to help out society and, if possible, make a difference in the entire world.

The Value of Education

In today's world, education is very crucial for one's success. Some might disagree and bring up how Steve Jobs and Bill Gates dropped out of college and became millionaires due to their inventions and ideas, but in reality the chances of being like them is one in a million. Therefore, we should get a full education and demonstrate to the youth that higher education is possible to reach.

As years pass by, the value of education tends to increase. Having a higher education gives people the ability to have a better life and not go through as many struggles and hardships that others might be facing. Furthermore, having a higher education or a college diploma allows for better jobs that will bring more money and allow for a better future that could possibly help change the world. As people, we must stand up together and graduate with a college degree to be a great example in the aspect that higher education can be achievable.

Writing Activity

1. Short-term goals are things you can accomplish in the near future and are often steps to long-term goals. Thus, long-term goals are goals that usually require time and effort, such as several short-term goals, to be completed first. What are your long-term goals? (for example: change the world, get a degree, be a community leader, etc.) Write a list of short-term goals that will help you get to a long-term goal (for example: make good grades, apply to scholarships, get involved in your community, etc.) You can achieve a lot when you have a clear plan!

2. What are your struggles and hardships? Write them down. How do you deal with them? Better yet, how will you overcome them? Write a poem about how your hardships can be overcome by you.

3. Who are some famous people you've heard of that accomplished great things? How did they accomplish them? Write a timeline of all the accomplishments you wish to achieve. Again, you can accomplish great things if you have a plan. Use your heroes as templates and accomplish great things on your terms.

K.J. Huey

K.J. Huey is 13 years old and shares the same birthday as Elvis Presley, but was born in 2002. She was born in Dallas, Texas and later moved to Longview, Texas. After eight years of living there, she moved to Nacogdoches. She loves to read, write, draw, listen to music, and increasing her flexibility. She grew up always loving to do those five things. But when it comes to writing and reading she never did like poetry. She has been told many times that her writing is like slam poetry, but she never did really see it or realize it.

K.J. grew up with hearing impairment and finally got hearing aids in 5th grade. She is her mother's oldest, but is the middle child on her father's side. She loves learning, using, and interpreting sign language in both English and ASL (American Sign Language). She and her wonderful sign language interpreter, Noelle Huether, from her church practice Christian songs in ASL and perform them in front of their church, First Church Of God in Nacogdoches, Texas, on Sundays. When Noelle isn't there to sign at church, her lovely daughter Corina Huether will sit next to her and type what pastor Lila Clay is saying on her laptop. Being told she was a gifted writer so often, she finally took the opportunity to attend Barrio Writers camp in 2015 and appreciates her ELA teacher, Angela Pliler, recommending this camp and the undying support of her amazing mother Dee Huey, family, and old friends.

Eyes

"Eyes can only see what they want when they're open-minded to the thought of getting hurt again. Beaten to the bone with the thought of all your worst events," —Built For Blame by Get Scared.

Some people say that our eyes are the windows to our souls and I believe that. I found a saying on a picture that says, "You're the girl with ghosts in her eyes." I believe that the eyes can tell you what a person is feeling inside and sometimes thinking. That doesn't always work though because stoic people tend to be really good at keeping their emotions a secret.

The eyes *can* only see what they want when they're open-minded to the thought of getting hurt again. If you ask me "what lies behind those pretty little eyes," I would, me being the goober I am, say, "A brain, duh."

The eyes are a tricky thing. They are very hard to understand. I know so because I have lived every day since I was 9 or 10 years old wishing that when asked how I am doing and I reply with an "I'm fine" every single time someone would finally look me in the eyes and say, "Tell me the truth."

Even the people who know me best actually believe it. They look at my face for just an instant and then go on with their lives, not even taking the time to search my eyes because my mouth was bent into a smile. When it comes to reading facial expressions or eyes, people can be so naïve and gullible. I'm the kind of person who looks into people's eyes and sees their souls. Even if someone looks happy or indifferent I know there is something wrong.

Being an ENFP personality type, Extrovert iNtuitive Feeling Prospecting, I have always had the ability to crack anyone's shell open. When I come across someone quiet, I always get them to talk to me and open up. Heh, I have yet to come across someone whose shell I *can't* crack.

Next time you ask someone how they are, look at their eyes for a few seconds. Don't just believe any answer you are given and only look at their eyes for a second or two.

Be careful, because it is hardly ever suspected that eyes can deceive and lie.

Acid, Violence and Emotions

You have no right to go spewing acid from your mouth and into people's ears. Words may not hurt you, but they do hurt many others. But what is worse than your fire is your actions. You may have heard of the phrase "Actions speak louder than words." It is very accurate and very true.

What you do mirrors what you are thinking or feeling inside even if you don't say anything about it. If you get into an argument with someone, verbal or physical or even both, one of you might use the saying, "Fists and skin could bruise me again but anything you say will only fuel my lungs."

I have no clue why, but for some reason the poison spat from a mouth hosting a forked tongue usually hurts so much more than the violence coming from a heated in-the-moment person. I have a theory though: it hurts worse because some people care and pay more attention to their emotions than their physical pain.

Some of you may not care about what I'm saying. Some of you may be indifferent to this. But to those of you who actually care about or relate to what I'm saying, I applaud you for your feelings. I congratulate you for actually listening to and believing some actual truth, for standing up for what is right. This reminds me of a quote from the singer of Black Veil Brides. "Stand up for what you believe in even if it means standing alone." — Andy Biersack.

Now, to those who don't really care about all this, I say to you, "Knowing that jellyfish have survived for 650 million years without brains gives some people hope."

This World is so Hateful

You've probably heard the song "Same Love" by Macklemore and Ryan Lewis ft. Mary Lambert (if not, look it up). Can you recall the most powerful and true words from that song? Macklemore sings, "In a world so hateful some would rather die than be who they are" and he is so, so, so very right. I know a few people who have tried to take their own life, knowing it wasn't theirs to take, because they were so sick and tired of being judged. Some failed and some . . . some of them are lost in time. We have got to stop stereotyping and judging others. Some of us even have the nerve to tell people to be who they are and then JUDGE those people. How sick and messed up is that? I know there are people in this room who have done the same thing. I know you will most likely deny it.

I pray and I hope and I have faith and I believe that this world can be turned around. I ask God to help me and the rest of his followers change people's thinking and beliefs. Not to necessarily change people who already have a faith or something that they believe in, but to change those who don't believe in anything. I want to reach out to people and give them something to believe in. But what I hope for most, what I wish for, what I ask for the most from God, is that this Earth's population as a whole will finally one day stop hating each other. It is killing me inside knowing that we judge and we hate each other but then we get all worked up and upset because someone was doing to us what we do to others. We are all a bunch of hypocrites. It hurts me so much seeing and knowing that people I know, love, dislike, and didn't even know existed are in so much pain and that many lay in bed contemplating their own death. Some plot the torment and murder of those who treated them so cruelly. There is not a single soul on this Earth who has respect for everyone and everything in this world. Not one and that is a sad fact. R-E-S-P-E-C-T. I give it to you, you give it to me and that is how it should be, but it doesn't work like that much anymore. What is even sadder is the fact that it is way too rare to find a human being that not only respects other Homo sapiens, but insects and animals too. We live on this Earth, right? Then why do you treat it like it is a landfill? We don't live in a dump, do we? No, we don't. It sure seems like it, though. Earth was not born a dumpster and it's purpose was not to be host to our mess because we are too lazy and careless to pick up ours and others' messes and to make sure that no more messes are made. When a piece of trash flies or drifts off of our picnic table we should stop what we are doing and go pick it up. We should throw it away, but I hardly ever see anyone do that. I do it and it upsets me deeply because I don't see anyone else doing it. Now, to get back on the topic of a world so hateful . . .

 I have tried to take my own life because I was so tired, angry, hurt, and empty from being drained by jerks who judged, hated, bullied, and assaulted my friends, family, loved ones, and people I didn't even know and got away with it. I failed, luckily. I forgot that my life wasn't mine to take and I didn't think I would be able to help people. We are killing each other's souls.

 I feel so dead inside. Empty. Emotionless. Do me a favor please. If you haven't heard these songs before then look up: "Gold" by Britt Nicole, "Another Empty Bottle" by Katy McAllister, "His Daughter" by Molly Kate Kestner, "Don't You Dare Forget The Sun" by Get Scared, "Built for Blame" by Get Scared, "Scars" by Say We Can Fly, "Love Note for a Rainy Day" by Saywecanfly, "Teenagers" by My Chemical Romance, "I'm Not Okay (I Promise)" by My Chemical Romance, "Brother" by Falling in Reverse, "Respect" by Aretha Franklin (or Melanie Amaro), "When She Cries" by Britt Nicole, "Kings and Queens" by Audio Adrenaline, "Held" by Natalie Grant, "The Real Me" by Natalie Grant, and "Brave" by Sara Bareilles. I hope they move you. I pray that they reach you.

Suicidal people, I am now talking directly to you. The reason you failed is because it is not your time yet. Your life is not yours to decide when it should be taken and it is not yours to take. God is NOT done with you yet. He created you for a purpose and he is not going to let you avoid fulfilling his plan. You are meant to still be here on this Earth. If someone tells you that you survived your attempt because you didn't try hard enough or didn't do it right . . . well, just remember: even though they are probably some of the biggest jerks this world has ever seen, Jesus still loves them. Let them know and I will blow their minds with my awesomeness way of words (no, I won't swear or cuss them out and I won't call them bad names). The Bible says that if you call someone a name or judge them then you are also judging yourself because you, too, do those same things.

I love the lyrics Ronnie Radke used in the song "Brother." Those words . . . so true. "No more laughs, no more hugs. So hold on to the ones you love." I found a quote on Google. It says, "Don't wait until it's too late to tell someone how much you love, how much you care. Because when they're gone, no matter how loud you shout and cry, they won't hear you anymore." Such accurate and powerful words. One last thing . . . when things are going badly and life is a mess, and you're wondering where God is, remember: the teacher is always quiet during the test.

"Scars and struggles on the way, but with joy our hearts can say. Yes, our hearts can say. Never once did we ever walk alone." —Never Once, by Matt Redman.

Writing Activity

1. What is your favorite music genre? What got you interested in that type of music? How different is it from the music your parents' listen to?

2. Have you ever had a piece of music change your life? What specifically changed you and why? Enough to write about it or use it as a reference like KJ did? If you haven't, just create a character or a piece of music that would cause such a thing to occur.

In Barrio Writers we say, "Your voice is your weapon!" It is how you can create change and defeat oppression. Write with those ideas in mind.

Judith Araziry

Judith Araziry was born an out-spoken girl on December 31, 1997. She was born healthy despite the doctors stating that, "Baby Judith will be born deaf and unable to speak." At the age of two, Judith started using her voice or as her mother would say, "habla asta por los codos". There was no doubt Judith would grow up to do wonderful things and empowering actions with her voice.

Judith is a young mujer that succeeds with her working hard and always improving anything she knows has not reached its full potential. This year is her third year at Barrio Writers and the reason she came back was because of her fantastic first experience she got to write with no restriction of grammar or spelling. She will continue to come back because she connected to her writing and to the environment better than any other space. Her experience also made her open up about the separation of her family due to the immigration system. On August 2009 when my mom was not able to show proper documentation she was deported to Mexico. They called her "illegal" and a menace to the United States, all though she had lived in the U.S. for many years and has a U.S. citizen daughter. Judith has been apart from her mom for 5 years now and about to graduate High school, wishing of having her mom at graduation. Judith has been part of Coyolxauhqui Circle for young wombyn, run by young wombyn and for young womybn where they developed their own zine. She was also part of, "Our Hood, Our Faces, and Our Voices" in Santa Ana where she presented her photography. Her live mission is to help her community. She teaches a public speaking class to girls between 5 and 10 years so that they can also find their voice. Judith started her own club at school called "Santa Ana Girl Up", that helps girls in developing countries with campaigns by the United Nations. Recently, she was awarded for her community work by the Soroptimist Violet Richardson award. Judith is an alumni of the Congressional Hispanic Caucus Institute and Hispanic National Bar Foundation Law Camp. Recently this summer she was chosen by her school to represent at California Girl State where she was awarded by Wellesley book, the Norton Book of Women's Lives award. Although, her life has been very rewarding, most of her strength stems from her life struggles that she has had to over come mostly on her own.

Two ribbons Tie from The Same String

Two ribbons tied
The story goes there was a gift
Two red pieces of string
One cut first
Followed by another
1st to be love
2nd to be care
The pieces were tied
By hands that were to give
1st ribbon for the person you love
2nd ribbon for the person you care for most
A mother found the pieces of sting
Tied them into ribbons to give
She thought of all in her heart
Listed the people for each ribbon apart
To whom she would give
and then she chose
She chose a girl
Who knew is who it have to be
She place both the love and care into
Hands that would learn to give
and softly spoke
"Tú mi niña mereces lo mejor
y esto es sólo un pequeño símbolo de nuestro amor"

La Casa de Mi Madre es Así

la casa de mi Madre es así
when you look through the window
you see no glass
not even to be let in with the danger of outside
almost ignorant
to the shadows of disaster that scream in alarm and rivers of blood that
innocents shed
it shield all by the protection of a lemon tree
la casa de mi Madre es así
ella lo entiende
worry is gone when the dangers of massacres and kidnappings are replaced
by the dangers of
los mosquitos
drinking your blood like a delicious
liquor
you can smell the food being prepared by the trees
falling on to the ground
la casa de mi Madre es así
if you compare the dirt under my feet
mine is darker
colder
blacker

her café
caliente
calmado

la casa de mi Madre es así
has a feel that sizes you like a lemon tree
bigger then the world as it shaped to become
only a memory
3 years now 5

la casa de mi Madre es así
the souls of the people who have none
iwonder
if they know the place they call home
if they think la casa de mi Madre es así

how do they explain that windows that must shield
using no glass because it has be broken
lemon tree can only protects if it watered
la casa de mi Madre es así
missing a core
mi casa is the same
i wonder only in memory as to how casa use to be
mi casa no asi
my home lacks the truth of un espíritu
the protection of a Lemon tree
los alimentos de Los aboles
de mi madre
le falta
le falto
me falta

Silence

a real speaker speaks
speaks, SPEAKS
shouts, whispers,
a real speaker relates does not just restate
shows does not tell
highlights and does not shield
real speaker speaks
speaks, SPEAKS
does not undermine to what he or she is opinionated
does not make less of what we know
or what we should be said
a real speaker speaks
speaks, SPEAKS
sometimes in the silence
we can't quite see nor hear
which is why we should all speak
why does the speaker stand in front?
to be seen
why does he or she?
if their ideas are traces to trade back
if a person is a speaker and can refer to what they have told

if the message is strong and can hold
than a real speaker speaks
speaks, SPEAKS
sees
beauty in their words
with no basis of dialect to their vocabulary
a real speaker speaks
speaks, SPEAKS
then is silence to listen
a real speaker speaks
speaks, SPEAKS
a merge of words and ideas
then is
then is
silenced
to listen
because a real speaker listens
listens LISTENS

Application Essay: Must be between 250-650 words

They asked me why I didn't come
If I had a reason
Sometimes I forget
Sometimes it is all news\
Sometimes all I wish it was just news
Something I could forget
Yet
Remember
Writing after
Believe their application would be incomplete without it

It felt I needed no explanation
Not having the need to explain where I was
And yet it affects me what if it hadn't been
Some students have a background, identity, interest, or talent
So they asked me to restate
Maybe I was fearful, aware, that I've grown up
Discuss an accomplishment or event, formal or informal that marked your

transition
From childhood to adulthood within your culture, community, or family
There is a new chapter in my life one that I am scared will now be as I planned
Then again I am prepared
I am aware that it wasn't planned sometimes
It's easy to believe others
They only lived with themselves and not their words
Bless their hearts if they were victim
Even if I was best
They're still testing me
Or is it that I am testing myself?
I am the teacher of my own teachings
Of which I want to learn
Sometimes I wish that I didn't know the unknown
Why then?
Is figuring it out hard
Alone?
You do everything by yourself
You cheer yourself up
You tear yourself down
You protect
You defend
You cry
You laugh
You don't cry
You can't cry
You don't laugh
You can't laugh
You sleep with your own thoughts
Your own thought keep you up
Be direct
Say it
It's great
Show don't tell
Please then share your story
How did that make you grow
Bring it back

Writing Activity

1. Have you undergone a moment in life that was very stressful and how did you overcome it? Write a reflection based on that experience and would you recommend to do different.
2. Write a response to Judith's piece, "Application Essay: Must be between 250-650 Words". Have you felt misunderstood by adults or the school system? Create a list and write your own experience through hip-hop, corrido, poetry, or essay form.

Alexa Smith

Alexa Smith was born on September 2nd, 1998 in Austin, Texas at the tender age of zero. She enjoys watching pretentious art films until she gets bored and switches to "Parks and Recreation." She hopes to one day be a screenwriter and use diversity and feminist ideals in her work to someday dismantle the patriarchy.

The Teacup

I didn't know the "B word" back then, but if I did I probably would have used it.

Or at least thought it.

The incident happened just days after my 10th birthday. Mountains of joy and celebration came tumbling down, my hopes and dreams broke along with that teacup. It started out innocently, two best friends making a tent that was to be enjoyed and cherished for as long as my mom allowed it to stay up. The construction was coming along wonderfully; sheets tied around chairs and blankets held in place on top of dressers with the heaviest of books.

But people run out of books. Tent construction this serious could not be stopped due to a mere shortage of books. We had to power on.

My best friend (who shall remain nameless) had the "brilliant" idea of using a box containing my beautiful, brand new, porcelain tea set in place of the books. She failed to ask me about this. Maybe if she had the whole fiasco could have been prevented. Instead she took it upon herself to place the tea set box on top of blankets in hopes of keeping them in place. Unfortunately, teacups and saucers are only so strong. The tea set's reign lasted mere minutes before it fell to the ground.

Only one teacup was harmed in the fall. Shattered with that teacup was not only my hopes and dreams but also our friendship.

Street Monsters

They lurk on the sides of streets, they yell and they shout and they whistle and they are soul crushingly loud. The stories your friends would tell you, with flashlights casting shadows across their faces, never involved anything this frightening. You thought you lost them a few blocks ago but there's more.

*

Monsters masquerading as construction workers. Instead of growling or biting they tell you how good your ass looks and all the different things they'd like to do to you.

You know they won't. You hope they won't.

*

You get to work and you think you're safe. You're boss can't be one of them, he has a wife and kids. But he grabs your ass as you walk in, and later comments on how your skirt looks a little slutty today. But it's all in good fun. All in good fun.

*

Your mom would never let you drive past 10 pm, because you were a young girl and the monsters go after young girls. But you realize now your age doesn't matter. The monsters are always there.

*

But they don't look like monsters. They look like your friends and your co-workers.
You can't believe them when they say they're one of the nice guys. Because the nice guys look just like the monsters.

Writing Activity
1. How would you define the term "Feminist"? Do you have to be a woman to be a feminist? Why or why not?

2. Read the definition for "patriarchy":

   Patriarchy: a system of society or government in which the father or eldest male is head of the family and descent is traced through the male line; a system of society or government in which men hold the power and women are largely excluded from it; a society or community organized on patriarchal lines.

3. Do you live in a patriarchal or matriarchal household? Create two columns, label one "patriarchy" and the second one "matriarchy," under each columns use single words to describe the title over the column. List up to 10 words within each column. Compare them, how are they similar or different? Then call them each a poem with the title over the words.

4. Research the link: **https://www.youtube.com/watch?v=0ze4AH_5kJw** on the internet. Watch the video titled, "Fighting Street Harassers With Confetti Guns And Punk Rock." How does this video connect with Alexa's piece "Street Monsters"? What other creative ways can women confront 'street monsters'? As a group, create your own response video to Alexa's collection of vignettes (short descriptions or stories)—then share it with us on the Barrio Writers Facebook!

Arnold Garcilazo

Arnold Garcilazo is a 16 year old from Garden Grove. He will enter his senior year of high school this year at Garden Grove High School. He is on his way to adulthood and is starting to take on responsibility every day. Just last year he thought he had things figured out but, is realizing that is not the case. He seems often to contradict himself in his poetry and statements. Although this seems difficult to understand life is often filled with the balance of opposites. Black and white, yin and yang, male and female, and everything else in between. Arnold is looking to better himself once again. He wants to prove to his parents that he is capable of doing great things. One thing he hopes to do is pay the house off for his parents so one day they no longer have to work. His biggest achievement thus far is getting a driving permit and a job, because this signifies his first steps into adulthood.

Ungrateful

I am ungrateful, I am greedy
I have everything I need and still want more
Ask myself, "What for?"
Shoes on my feet, clothes on my back
Food and a home, what do I lack?
Mom and dad had much less
And still managed to find happiness

Material tempts me, although I try my best
Maybe it's God's test
I see gold chains, gold watches, fast cars, big houses
And just hope one day I have it all
What will it matter when I fall six feet deep?
Material is just the devil calling out to me
I make mistakes, but I'm in a position to see
My ambitions are greater than my decisions

Young Brown Male

Society sees a young brown male
Son of immigrants so he will never prevail
His use of language is explicit and graphic
The way he wears his garments untraditional
Pierced ears, so tattoos must be next
Who are they to speak on my behalf
They can't fit the shoes I walk in
Police officers see a criminal, a vandal
Teachers see an uneducated, obnoxious child
Donald Trump sees a rapist, murderer
Labels get thrown around and stereotypes are formed
One things for sure they don't know who I am
And I don't know either
After being labeled so much you start to question yourself
and wonder if the stereotypes are real
If people stopped being so judgmental
and closed minded
I would know who I am

Writing Activity
1. Every day is a journey. Sometimes it's easy to disregard its existence. Do you have a routine life? If so how do you go about defining it before it escapes you? If not, when do you when do you reflect on the days that have past?

2. Have there been any labels attached to you or your community? Among your group, do a circle map of all the labels and together write a collective piece that counters the labels attached to your community.

Shyla Driver

Shyla Driver was born in Nacogdoches, Texas on July 22, 2001. Now at age 13, she is going to attend Nacogdoches High School as a freshman. She lives with her mother, father, younger sister, and her dog.

Shyla suffers from frequent migraines, which are triggered by many things. Despite this, she still makes good grades and participates in her school Band and Model United Nations club. She hopes to become a screenplay writer and wants to attend the Juilliard School of Fine Arts in New York.

One Touch

Our legs pressed together at our own accord
The look on our faces showed we were utterly bored
But I felt such a sensation at this casual touch
I had never felt this; it was almost too much
I notice his hand had landed on my knee
I guess the next move was supposed to be me…

Every Shooting Star

Every shooting star
is a dream
a crazy, wicked outrageous dream
that comes true.

Like a boy, poorer than dirt
who makes it to the NFL.
Or a woman
who goes from a prostitute to a performer.
"And still I rise."

I've never seen a shooting star.
They're there
I've just
missed them all.

Wish on every dandelion,
fallen eyelash,
birthday candle,
every shooting star
and lay your hopes upon it.
Drop an anvil on a feather, please!

Every shooting star
will always
die out on me.

<u>Writing Activity</u>
1. What are some challenges in your life? How do they make it difficult for you to accomplish daily life, get good grades or just wake up in the morning? What are some ways you overcome them?

2. With your goals in mind, what type of advice would you give someone who is two years younger than you? What would you prepare to be ready to face what you are facing? Now, write a letter to your younger self, giving yourself advice. Sharing the good and bad of what you have faced and how you still keep pursing your dreams.

3. Write a letter to your future self, maybe 5 or 10 years from now (or maybe just to your graduate self, after middle school or high school or college graduation). Don't share it. Save it. Put it in an envelope with a date 5 or 10 years (after graduation) from now. Then in 5 or 10 years (after graduation) open it, read it, compare it to how you feel at that moment.

Galilea Marcos

Galilea Marcos, 16 year-old mostly known as "gali," is a young xhicana activist fighting to stop police brutality. Living with her supportive parents, one chingon hermano, two powerful sisters and two beautiful healthy dogs. She was born in Santa Ana until she moved to Garden Grove and now she's back into her barrio Santa Ana.

During her 8th year in middle school she dealt with police issues. One day walking home she got pulled over by a cop with her brother and his girlfriend. A friend of her had recorded the whole incident and told her that they should file a report. They filed a report to the Santa Ana Police Department and ended up getting to the Santa Ana Unified School District. Her parents later got threats from the district saying they needed to stop all this because they were going to end up losing. That's when she started getting involved into these organizations in her community that address police brutality and also how to deal with police encounters as a youth, parent, or undocumented. She gives workshops on knowing your rights to youth parents and even college students. She knew she had to speak up about police issues as a young youth.

Gali is also part of a young womyn circle known as Coyolxauhqui where they are able to empower one another and fight for the destruction of patriarchy. Also in love with the show East Los High that address H.I.V., teen pregnancy, domestic violence, immigration, police brutality, and LGBTQ+ issues. She also believes we come from corn.

La Calle Cuatro

Walking down the streets of 4th street hearing señoras y señores yelling to come into their stores. Seeing people sell fruta, mangonadias, Cheetos, dulce, just across the street. Holding the soft warm hands of my ama making sure I don't run across the street. Buying a helado just right next to the carousel and tasting the cold sweet helado de limón. I remember touching the carousel and hearing the sounds of happy kids just like me. Yes I do miss the carousel, yes I do miss the nice sweet helado de limón and I wouldn't have to miss them if this was still 4th street.

Dear Future Me

Dear future me,

Remember to be free
Remember you were a little G

Remember to keep spreading peace

Remember to empower others

Remember to fight for what's right

Remember your roots

Remember your familia

Remember those who helped you out through your struggle
Remember the streets of the OC

Oh and remember fuck the police.

Mi Casa

My parents running up to me telling me we have to move as soon as we can never picture it was going to be that same day. I already knew I was moving but I thought we had a month dam this is going to be a bust. Parents screaming rushing out the door with boxes and stuff and me asking myself what have they done? My mind is everywhere at this point I don't even know how to feel. Should I feel mad, sad, I don't even know. We are running out of time we have to leave before 3. Can they just stop and breathe? The last box to carry out the door please hold the door. Walking, down the step of the front door my parents yelling at me to hurry. Getting inside the car ready to leave is this really how it's going to be? Car starts pulling away looking out the window one last time and enjoying the view of mi casa and saying to myself, "no me quero ir."

My Senses

I would be a bird they are able to be free and that's something I want to be free. I can fly and go wherever I want to go without any one stopping me and my dreams.

The sun was orange red and not that bright. It was touching the horizon of the beach while people on the boats waving hi to me. A seal is laying down right next to the big rock across my eyes just staring at me. A nice ocean breeze passing through me.

My Amas cocina no esta cochina. Touching the stove and feeling that little bit of jugo de frijoles she dropped. Her mandlin hanging right next to the frutas and seeing the sink squeaky clean. Smelling the fresh made tortillas.

Galilea, gali, golly, coletas, flaca, mocosa, punk, kid, cabrona, yup that's me.

Make a Hip Hop song about me make sure its goes with me. Maybe you should name it after me.

Police Brutality

We need to start addressing police brutality by taking it to the streets and demanding for peace. Not just asking for it but fighting for justice and equality. We need to be able to stand together like a communidad and end these killings, beatings, shootings. We can't let the color of our own skin, blood, culture, ethnicity, where we live define us. We define ourselves.

We need to make these people with power listen to our demand because we are tires of their oppressive system. Make banners, posters, make lots of noise scream in the streets if you have too but don't apologize for your anger please don't apologize make them realize that this system they call "helpful" has destroyed half of us. We won't stand down because the people are stronger than the people in power.

Youth and Adults

Youth are stupid, adults are smart
Youth are uneducated, adults are educated
Youth are rebels, adults are at peace
Youth are uncontrollable, adults are calm
Youth are ignorant, adults are rational
Somos los mocosos y ellos son los que Mandan.
Adults say we are a messed up generation but who made this generation?
When we want to speak up we can't because we are ignorant mocosos/mocosas.
We as youth matter and our voice will be heard by our family's and the people in power.
We won't get put down by these youth stereotypes
Because we are young mococos/mocosas with a voice that will be heard.

Writing Activity

1. Gali's writing is very powerful and yet playful, focus on her first piece "La Calle Cuatro," what stands out to you? Notice how she uses two languages and a childhood memory to create an image? As a reader, do you like it? Why or why not?

2. Think about your own childhood, is there a specific language in your family that is used? Maybe nicknames or sayings only your family uses, maybe a different language or personal references. Now, also add a special place and food that reminds you of your childhood, maybe a place that no longer exist like the carousel on 4th Street that Gali references. Write your own memory—what is your nostalgia?

   > **Nostalgia:** nos·tal·gia, *noun*, a sentimental longing or wistful affection for the past, typically for a period or place with happy personal associations.

Phoenix Conditt

Phoenix Conditt was born in 2002 in Nacogdoches, Texas. He currently attends Mike Moses Middle School and is going to the 8th grade. He has previously won 5th place District Champion in UIL Spelling and 3rd place in UIL Dictionary Skills.

Forever No One

I am like any other teen.
I go to school. I get bullied.
I learn from mistakes. I participate
In UIL contests. I do chores at home.
I deal with bad acne and other disgusting
Shit. I lift weights and stretch and run
In athletics class. I do homework wishing
Such a damn thing as math never existed.
And then I go to bed and pretend nothing
Ever happened.
I am no one.

But what people don't realize is that
When they say that no one is perfect
They are saying that anyone who is no
One, like me, can be perfect.

So if you say that you are no one
And there's nothing to do about it,
That is a good thing. You can learn
To be perfect. You can learn to get up,
Make a change, and go make a difference
In people's lives. You can change
The world without not trying to be no one.

So if I am no one,
And no one really cares,
. . .
I am proud of who I am.
And you can be proud of being no one, too.

Writing Activity
1. After reading Phoenix's piece aloud, discuss how he redefines the term "no one." Have you ever referred to someone as "no one," have you ever been treated like a "no one"? How is this a form of bullying or oppression?

   > **Oppression:** *noun,* the state of being subject to unjust or unfair treatment.

2. Barrio Writers chooses to reclaim the word "barrio." Similarly, Phoenix chose to reclaim the term "no one." For example, across the U.S. people associate the word "barrio" with "ghetto" or a bad neighborhood filled with Latinos. What type of neighborhood is a "ghetto," how can this term be reclaimed? When/where was this word first used? Do some research on "ghetto," then discuss how it came to be used negatively.

3. There are several words that we use regularly that can be changed from negative to positive. Based on your personal experiences, choose a word/term you want to reclaim and turn positive as Phoenix did with his piece. Try an acrostic poem or just a rant writing what the word/term means to you.

   > An **acrostic poem** is a type of poetry where the first, last or other letters in a line spell out a particular word or phrase. The

most common and simple form of an acrostic poem is where the first letters of each line spell out the word or phrase.

Example — An acrostic poem using "Barrio Writers"

Bold youth
Are what our world needs
Replacing oppression with empowerment
Replacing stereotypes with success
Including youth everyday
Offering them their own space

Worthy of titles like "author" and "scholar"
Remembering one day they will grow up to be our leaders
Investing in their words
Telling them they matter
Expecting them to be more than the media headlines
Respecting their ideas
So they to have a chance to feel pride before they feel rejection.

Marilynn Montaño

Marilynn Montaño is a young Chicana poet, writer, community organizer, and proud daughter to migrant parents from Puebla, Mexico. Since the age of fifteen, she has been active in her city through spoken word, community organizing, and documenting life by any means necessary. Her writing has been featured in *Mujeres de Maiz, Santanero Zine, Seeds of Resistance Zine, Barrio Writers,* and *Los Angeles Water Works: Histories of Water and Place*. Montano's journalistic writing work has been published in *The Orange County Register, Voice of OC,* and *OC Weekly.* In 2013, she received the "OC Press Club Award". Currently, she is the Orange County Program Director for *Barrio Writers* and coordinated The People's Data Project in collaboration with The Kennedy Commission and El Centro Cultural de Mexico in result of publishing the "Lacy in Crisis and Action" report. When Marilynn is not writing or community organizing she enjoys watching stationery videos on Youtube and sipping on Café de Olla from Café Calacas.

Dear Chula con Writer's Block,

A while ago, your voice and words synced so nicely in between your hands
You let your glow be heard with all the emotions and words
You promised yourself *chula* that you would not let yourself down
See them petals came out so smooth

Rhythm running down your legs every full moon
Why did you let yourself go?
Soon bus rides became just bus rides
Mornings became afternoons
Yet, you still struggle to accept the world as yours, *chula*
If you just let yourself own it!
Why must you keep denying yourself, *chula*?
Tu eres la mejor fuerza de mi vida
Now, I ask you, why did you the negativity consume your *chulada* spirit?
    fears
    self-doubt
    eating disorder
Times may be tough, but let your *chulada* fucking shine mujer!
Cuz who else knows who you are *chula*?
Underneath all those scattered journals
It's you, la luna con su noche
Who gives meaning
    piesitos
    trekking through the chaotic
    delicate ground of past and present
Your fear underneath your hard bed
Shadows on discolored walls
It doesn't belong to you
    Let it go
    Let yourself be
There is already enough injustices around you *chulada*
You're the temple y la fuerza
Tue eres movimiento
You're a *chulada*, underneath those forgotten pages
That vision board adorned with a cap and gown and poetry
Those discolored walls belong to you, cover them with dreams
    They are still yours
    So please
    Let yourself be
Sincerely,
La Chula

Our Barrios, Our Borders

This poem goes out to our 'hoods where they say it ain't changing but look around it keeps (re)arranging without consent from the people. Donde están nuestros vecindarios?

In between Santa Ana and Garden Grove
nothing permanent
Un cuarto rentado to another "room for rent" sign
between $800 to $1500
Never enough
92701, 92703, 92704, 92706
Zip codes pushing
Reinforcing struggles
while papá se machuca las manos at work

In downtown
overpriced artisan bread
hand-crafted beer
spiked up parking prices
New overpriced juice bar
where my amá will never walk into
porque she can only afford la comida de casa

Pricing us out of our homes so they can kill us in the streets
Raising rents, making it impossible to survive
This city is cuffing our colored brothers and sisters
gang injunction zones ready to clean up our barrios
and throw away las llaves

These pro-gentrification plans dressed up in foreign words
my parents do not even understand
They feel it in their bones
They always gotta work to live and live to work

"Cuanto cuesta eso?"
The cringe in my parents' faces
The system keeps cheating them out
Reinventing their place in society
Borders stretched, people displaced

Our barrios, sacred spaces without a home

Writing Activity
1. Are you a writer? Do you ever feel stuck when you are writing? Free write to the last conversation you had at school or at home.

    Free writing is a prewriting practice in which a person writes without stopping for a set period of time (try 10-15 minutes), don't worry about spelling, grammar, or topic. It produces raw pieces—"throw up on paper" as we say in Barrio Writers—but helps writers overcome blocks of hesitation and self-criticism.

2. Take a tour with your group of your city's downtown and compare to your neighborhood. Is your city's downtown beautified and clean? How many libraries does your city have? How does gentrification affect the economy for low-income families? Write your own version of what you found out and how does it make you feel?

    Gentrification: renovate and improve (especially a house or district) so that it conforms to middle-class taste.

    Economy: the wealth and resources of a country or region, especially in terms of the production and consumption of goods and services.

www.ingramcontent.com/pod-product-compliance
Lightning Source LLC
Chambersburg PA
CBHW020407080526
44584CB00014B/1210